Table of Contents

5

Chapter 1: Introduction to Godot

1.1 Understanding Godot and Its Capabilities

Godot is a powerful, open-source game engine used for the development of 2D and 3D games. One of the key features that set Godot apart is its scene and node architecture. In Godot, everything is a node. A scene is a collection of nodes organized in a hierarchical manner. This flexible structure allows for highly modular and reusable design patterns.

Each node in Godot has its specific purpose and functionality. For instance, a Sprite node is used for 2D graphics, while a Camera node is vital for 3D rendering. The ability to combine and configure these nodes offers immense creative freedom to developers.

Another significant aspect of Godot is its dedicated scripting language, GDScript. GDScript is a high-level, dynamically typed programming language closely integrated with the engine. It is designed to be easy to learn and use, with a syntax similar to Python. For example, here is a simple GDScript code snippet that moves a node:

```
extends Node2D

func _process(delta):
    position.x += 100 * delta
```

This code extends a Node2D, which is a common node for 2D games, and uses the _process function to update the node's position. The delta parameter represents the elapsed time since the last process call, ensuring smooth movement regardless of frame rate.

Godot also supports visual scripting, a node-based system that lets developers create game logic visually. This is particularly beneficial for those who prefer not to delve into traditional coding.

The engine is equipped with a robust animation system, allowing for the creation of intricate animations. Godot's animation tools are not limited to character or object movements; they can also animate properties, call methods, and even trigger signals.

In terms of graphics, Godot provides a versatile renderer supporting both 2D and 3D games. The 3D engine features advanced rendering techniques, including physically based rendering (PBR), dynamic lighting, shadows, and post-processing effects. The 2D engine is no less powerful, with support for sprites, animations, particle systems, and more.

Godot's physics engine offers both 2D and 3D physics, enabling realistic motion and collisions. It includes support for various physics bodies, areas, and joints, allowing for the creation of complex physical interactions.

One of the most appealing aspects of Godot is its cross-platform capability. Games developed in Godot can be exported to numerous platforms, including Windows, macOS, Linux, Android, iOS, and HTML5, with minimal platform-specific adjustments.

Godot's asset pipeline is also worth mentioning. It supports a range of file formats and provides tools for importing, optimizing, and managing game assets. This feature is especially useful for teams collaborating on game development.

The Godot community plays a vital role in the engine's development and growth. Being open-source, it has a thriving community that contributes to its codebase, creates plugins, writes documentation, and offers support through forums and social media.

In conclusion, Godot's combination of powerful features, ease of use, and community support makes it an excellent choice for both beginner and experienced game developers. Its ability to handle a wide range of game development tasks, from scripting to rendering to physics simulation, positions it as a versatile and capable game engine.

1.2 The History of Godot and Open-Source Game Engines

The history of Godot is a fascinating journey that mirrors the evolution of the gaming industry and open-source software development. Godot, initially developed in-house by Juan Linietsky and Ariel Manzur for several commercial games, was released as open-source software in February 2014. This marked a significant shift in the game development landscape, as it was one of the first full-featured, open-source game engines made available to the public.

The decision to open-source Godot was driven by a desire to contribute to the gaming community and a belief in the collaborative power of open-source development. The founders recognized the limitations of proprietary game engines, particularly for independent developers and small studios who often lacked the resources to access high-quality tools.

Upon its release, Godot's source code was made available on GitHub, inviting developers worldwide to contribute and improve upon the engine. This move rapidly accelerated its development, as volunteers started to enhance its features, fix bugs, and create documentation.

One of the key milestones in Godot's history was the introduction of GDScript. The developers of Godot saw the need for a scripting language that was easy to use and optimized for the engine. GDScript, inspired by Python's syntax, was thus created. This scripting language became a core component of Godot, offering a user-friendly yet powerful way to script game logic.

```
# A simple GDScript function
func say_hello(name):
    print("Hello, " + name)
```

As Godot matured, it began to attract attention not only from hobbyists but also from professional game developers. Its capability to handle both 2D and 3D game development, coupled with its cross-platform support, made it a versatile option for various projects.

The engine's 3D capabilities, while initially less advanced than its 2D features, have seen significant improvements over the years. The introduction of physically based rendering (PBR), advanced lighting, and shadow effects brought Godot closer in line with other major game engines.

In parallel to its technical advancements, Godot's community grew exponentially. Online forums, social media groups, and annual conferences fostered a sense of community and collaboration. This community has been instrumental in driving Godot's development, offering support to new users, creating tutorials, and even developing third-party extensions.

Godot's version history is marked by significant releases that introduced new features and improvements. For instance, Godot 3.0, released in January 2018, brought a new renderer, improved physics engine, and C# support, broadening its appeal.

The engine's approach to project management and scene construction also sets it apart from other engines. Godot treats scenes as reusable components, making it easier to build complex games from modular, manageable pieces. This approach simplifies the development process, especially for teams.

One of the challenges Godot faced in its early years was performance optimization. However, through continuous development and community contributions, these issues have been largely addressed, resulting in a more efficient and robust engine.

Godot's commitment to remaining free and open-source is a core part of its philosophy. Unlike some other engines, Godot does not impose royalties or licensing fees, making it an attractive option for independent developers and educational institutions.

In recent years, Godot has also made strides in supporting virtual reality (VR) and augmented reality (AR) development, areas that are becoming increasingly important in the gaming industry.

The engine's development has been guided by regular feedback from its user base. The developers of Godot maintain an open dialogue with the community, ensuring that updates and new features align with the needs and wishes of its users.

Looking ahead, Godot's roadmap includes further enhancements to its 3D engine, better integration with various platforms, and continued refinement of GDScript. The engine's developers are also focused on improving documentation and educational resources, making it more accessible to newcomers.

In conclusion, Godot's journey from an in-house game engine to a prominent open-source platform is a testament to the power of community-driven development. Its continual evolution, guided by the needs of its users and the contributions of its community, has established it as a key player in the world of game development.

1.3 Setting Up Godot: Installation and Basic Configuration

Setting up Godot is a straightforward process, designed to be accessible for users of all levels. The first step is to download the Godot engine from its official website. Godot offers several versions, including standard and Mono versions (for C# support). It's important to choose the one that best fits your development needs.

Once downloaded, Godot does not require a traditional installation process. The downloaded file is a self-contained executable, meaning you can run it directly without going through an installation wizard. This portability is a significant advantage, allowing developers to keep different versions of the engine or move their development environment easily.

For Windows users, simply downloading the .exe file and running it will open the Godot editor. On macOS, after downloading the .dmg file, you need to drag the Godot icon to the Applications folder. Linux users, depending on their distribution, will typically download a .zip or .tar.gz file and can run the executable directly from the extracted folder.

Upon launching Godot for the first time, you'll be greeted with the Project Manager. This interface is where you create new projects or open existing ones. To start a new project, click on 'New Project', enter a name, choose a location on your filesystem for the project, and specify a renderer (OpenGL ES 3.0 for higher-end graphics or OpenGL ES 2.0 for wider compatibility).

Configuring the editor settings is the next step. Godot allows extensive customization of the editor interface, including theme, font size, and interface language. This customization can be accessed through the Editor Settings in the top menu.

```
# Example: Changing the default script editor font size
EditorSettings.set("text_editor/font_size", 14)
```

Godot also offers a project settings window, which is crucial for configuring your game's properties. Here, you can set the window size, enable or disable features, and configure platform-specific options. This window is accessible through the 'Project' menu in the editor.

The asset library is another essential feature in Godot. It allows you to browse, download, and install add-ons, plugins, and assets directly from the editor. This can significantly speed up the development process by providing ready-made solutions for common needs.

For those interested in scripting with C#, setting up Mono in Godot is an additional step.

1.4 Navigating the Godot Interface: Key Features and Tools

Navigating the Godot interface efficiently is crucial for a streamlined game development process. The interface is divided into several key areas, each serving a specific purpose in the game development workflow.

The centerpiece of the Godot interface is the Editor Viewport. This area displays the current scene, allowing developers to place and manipulate nodes. In 3D mode, it provides a three-dimensional view of the scene, while in 2D mode, it presents a flat canvas for 2D game development.

Adjacent to the Editor Viewport is the Scene Panel. This panel displays the hierarchy of nodes in the current scene. It is where you can organize the structure of your game elements, parent nodes to each other, and select individual nodes for editing.

The Inspector Panel, located typically on the right side of the interface, is where you can view and modify the properties of the selected node. Properties might include positional data, visual aspects, scripts, and custom variables, among others.

Below the viewport is the FileSystem Dock. It provides a view of your project's file structure, allowing you to organize, rename, and manage your game's files and folders. This includes scripts, scenes, assets, and any other resources you've added to your project.

The Toolbar at the top of the viewport offers quick access to various tools and functionalities. This includes options for running the game, debugging, and scene manipulation tools like move, rotate, and scale, which are essential for scene creation.

The Script Editor is a key feature for those who will be scripting in Godot. It supports syntax highlighting, code completion, and debugging tools. The editor is designed to work seamlessly with GDScript, though it also supports other languages like C# if you're using the Mono version of Godot.

```
# Sample GDScript function in the Script Editor
func _ready():
    print("Hello, Godot!")
```

For 2D development, Godot offers a comprehensive set of tools in the 2D view. These include tools for creating and manipulating sprites, tilemaps, and animations. The editor also provides robust support for 2D physics, making it easy to add realistic movement and collisions to your game.

In 3D development, the 3D view comes with tools for importing models, setting up materials and shaders, and configuring lights and cameras. Godot's 3D engine supports advanced features like PBR, shadows, and post-processing effects, which are all accessible from within the 3D editor.

The Animation Editor in Godot is a powerful tool that allows for the creation of complex animations.

1.5 The Godot Community: Resources and Support

The Godot community is a vibrant and essential aspect of the Godot experience. This community consists of developers, artists, designers, and enthusiasts who contribute to the growth and improvement of the Godot engine. There are various resources and platforms where the community interacts, shares knowledge, and offers support.

One of the primary places for community interaction is the official Godot website and forums. Here, users can find a wealth of information, ask questions, share experiences, and get feedback on their projects. The forums are segmented into categories like general discussion, project showcase, and help and support, making it easy to find relevant conversations.

Godot also has an official documentation site, which is an invaluable resource for developers of all skill levels. The documentation covers everything from basic tutorials to advanced features, and it's regularly updated by community members. It's a great place to start for anyone new to Godot or looking to expand their knowledge.

```
# Example of a commonly shared script in community forums
func _ready():
    print("This is a basic Godot script shared in the community!")
```

The Q&A section on the Godot website is another essential resource. It's a platform where users can ask specific questions and get answers from experienced members of the community. This section is especially useful for solving particular problems or getting advice on best practices.

Godot's community is also active on social media platforms like Twitter, Reddit, and Facebook. These platforms host discussions, news updates, and community events. They are also great places for networking and connecting with other Godot developers.

Discord and IRC channels dedicated to Godot provide real-time communication among community members. These channels are often used for quick questions and answers, as well as informal discussions about game development with Godot.

2.2 Scripting in Godot: An Introduction to GDScript

GDScript is Godot's native scripting language, designed specifically for the engine. It is a high-level, dynamically typed language that is heavily inspired by Python. This means it is not only powerful but also easy to learn, especially for those who have experience with Python.

The primary purpose of GDScript is to provide an efficient way to define the behavior of game elements. Every node in a Godot scene can have a GDScript attached to it, allowing it to perform specific actions, respond to events, and interact with other nodes.

One of the first concepts to understand in GDScript is the use of functions. Functions in GDScript are blocks of code that perform a specific task. The most common function used in

Godot scripting is the _ready() function, which is called when a node is added to the scene tree.

```
func _ready():
    print("Node has been added to the scene!")
```

This function can be used to initialize variables, set up node properties, or start processes that need to happen when the node starts.

Another important function is the _process(delta) function. This function is called every frame and is where you would handle things like movement or other frame-dependent actions.

```
func _process(delta):
    position.x += 10 * delta
```

In this example, the position of the node is updated every frame, creating a movement effect.

Variables in GDScript can be declared and used to store values. Variables can be of various types such as integers, strings, or more complex types like arrays and dictionaries.

```
var health = 100
var player_name = "Godot Ninja"
```

These variables can then be used within functions or to share data between different parts of your script.

GDScript also supports control flow statements such as if, else, while, and for. These are used to perform different actions based on conditions or to iterate over collections.

```
if health > 0:
    print("Player is alive")
else:
    print("Player is defeated")
```

This example checks the player's health and prints a message based on the condition.

Signals are a key feature of GDScript and Godot, allowing nodes to communicate with each other. Signals can be emitted and connected to functions, which are then called when the signal is emitted.

```
signal player_died

func _ready():
    connect("player_died", self, "_on_Player_died")

func _on_Player_died():
    print("Player has died")
```

In this case, a signal `player_died` is emitted and connected to a function that handles the player's death.

GDScript also supports inheritance, allowing you to create scripts that extend the functionality of other scripts. This is useful for creating general behaviors that can be extended or modified in specific instances.

Error handling in GDScript is done using the `assert` keyword or by handling exceptions using `try`, `catch`, and `finally` blocks.

GDScript integrates seamlessly with the Godot editor, providing features like auto-completion, syntax highlighting, and inline error checking, which makes writing and debugging scripts much easier.

For those who prefer a visual approach, Godot also offers VisualScript, a node-based scripting language. VisualScript is especially useful for artists or designers who might not be comfortable with traditional coding.

For more advanced users, Godot also supports C# scripting, providing the power of a statically typed language. C# scripts can be used alongside GDScript, giving developers more flexibility in their choice of language.

In conclusion, GDScript is a powerful yet user-friendly language that provides the necessary tools for scripting in Godot. Its integration with the engine, coupled with features like signals and inheritance, makes it an ideal choice for both beginners and experienced programmers working on Godot projects.

2.3 Visual Scripting: An Alternative to Coding

Visual Scripting in Godot is an alternative approach to traditional text-based scripting, offering a more intuitive way for certain developers, especially those with a visual or design background, to contribute to game logic and behavior. It allows the creation of scripts using a graphical interface, where nodes and connections represent the flow of the program.

The core concept of Visual Scripting in Godot revolves around a node-based system. Each node in a visual script represents a function, variable, or control flow statement. These nodes are connected by wires, which define the flow of data and execution within the script.

To get started with Visual Scripting, you first need to attach a Visual Script to a node in your scene. This is done in a similar way to attaching a GDScript, but instead of writing code, you'll be working in the Visual Scripting editor.

The Visual Scripting editor in Godot is split into two main areas: the node palette and the workspace. The node palette contains a list of available nodes, categorized by their function. The workspace is where you drag and drop nodes and connect them together to build your script.

Basic operations, like arithmetic or logic comparisons, are performed using nodes specifically designed for these tasks. For example, you can use an 'Add' node to add two numbers, or an 'If' node to perform a conditional check.

```
# Example: Adding two numbers using Visual Script
[Add Node] -> [Output Node]
```

In this example, an 'Add' node would be used to add two input values, with the result being passed to an output node.

Variables in Visual Scripting are represented by 'Set' and 'Get' nodes. These nodes allow you to store and retrieve values, similar to variables in traditional scripting languages.

Control flow in Visual Scripting, such as loops and conditionals, is handled using nodes like 'For', 'While', or 'If'. These nodes control the execution flow based on their conditions or parameters.

```
# Example: Conditional logic using Visual Script
[If Node] -> [Do Something] -> [Else Do Something Else]
```

In this example, an 'If' node directs the flow to different branches based on a condition.

Visual Scripting also supports the use of signals.

2.4 The Node System: Hierarchies and Dependencies

Understanding the node system in Godot is crucial for effectively developing games using the engine. Nodes are the basic building blocks of a Godot project, and understanding how they interact and depend on each other is key to leveraging the full power of the engine.

In Godot, everything in a scene is a node. Nodes can represent a wide range of elements, from visual objects like sprites and lights to logic-based elements like scripts and timers. Each node has a specific function and set of properties that define its behavior.

Nodes are organized into a tree-like hierarchy. In this hierarchy, one node can be the parent of one or more child nodes. This parent-child relationship is fundamental to how Godot structures scenes and objects within them.

The hierarchical nature of nodes allows for an organized and modular approach to game development. For example, in a player character scene, the parent node might be a KinematicBody2D, with children nodes for the sprite, collision shape, and camera.

```
# Example of setting up a node hierarchy in GDScript
var player = KinematicBody2D.new()
var sprite = Sprite.new()
player.add_child(sprite)
```

In this example, a player character is created with a sprite as a child, illustrating the parent-child relationship.

Each node in the hierarchy inherits properties and transforms from its parent. This means that if you move, rotate, or scale a parent node, its children will follow suit. This inheritance is powerful for creating complex objects that move and act as a single unit.

Godot's node system is designed to be flexible. Nodes can be added, removed, or rearranged at runtime, allowing for dynamic changes to the scene tree. This can be used for things like spawning enemies, creating procedural levels, or building interactive UIs.

```
# Example of adding a node at runtime
var enemy = EnemyScene.instance()
get_node("Enemies").add_child(enemy)
```

In this example, an enemy node is instantiated and added to the scene tree dynamically.

Each node type in Godot comes with a set of functionalities specific to its purpose. For instance, a Timer node can emit a signal after a set amount of time, while an AnimationPlayer node can play animations.

Understanding signals and how they work with nodes is another crucial aspect. Signals are a way for nodes to communicate with each other. For example, a button node can emit a signal when it's pressed, and any other node can connect to this signal to react to the button press.

Dependency among nodes is not just limited to parent-child relationships. Nodes can also reference other nodes elsewhere in the scene tree, allowing for complex interactions and behaviors.

One common challenge in working with node hierarchies is maintaining a clear and manageable structure, especially in larger projects. Proper naming conventions and organization are key to keeping the scene tree understandable.

Godot's scene system complements the node hierarchy. Scenes can be saved and instanced as nodes, making it easy to reuse components across your game. For example, you could create a scene for an enemy and instance it multiple times in your levels.

In terms of performance, understanding how to optimize node hierarchies is important. Unnecessary nodes or overly complex hierarchies can impact the performance of your game, especially on lower-end hardware.

The Godot editor provides tools to visualize and edit node hierarchies, making it easier to understand and manage the structure of your scenes. This includes features like the Scene Dock, where you can see the tree structure of your current scene, and the Inspector, where you can edit the properties of selected nodes.

For advanced users, Godot offers the ability to create custom node types via scripting. This allows for extending the engine's functionality and creating specialized nodes for specific tasks.

Debugging issues related to node hierarchies can sometimes be challenging, especially when dealing with complex interactions. Godot's debugging tools, such as the remote scene tree inspector, can be invaluable in these situations.

In conclusion, the node system is a core feature of the Godot engine, providing a flexible and powerful framework for building games. Understanding node hierarchies and dependencies is essential for anyone looking to develop games with Godot, whether they are a beginner or an experienced developer.

2.5 Project Management: Organizing

Chapter 3: 2D Game Development

3.1 Creating 2D Worlds: Sprites, Tiles, and Backgrounds

In 2D game development with Godot, creating engaging and visually appealing worlds is crucial. This involves the use of sprites, tilesets, and backgrounds to build immersive environments for players to explore.

Sprites are the basic visual elements in any 2D game. In Godot, a sprite is typically a 2D image that can be manipulated and animated within the game world. Godot's Sprite node is used to represent these images.

3.2 Animations and Effects in 2D

Animations and effects play a crucial role in 2D game development, adding dynamism and polish to the game experience. In Godot, there are various tools and techniques available for creating engaging animations and visual effects.

The AnimationPlayer node is one of the primary tools for creating animations in Godot. It allows for the sequencing of various properties over time, such as position, rotation, scale, and even frame changes for sprite animations. This node is extremely flexible and can animate almost any property of any node.

```
# Example: Animating a sprite using AnimationPlayer
var animation = Animation.new()
animation.add_track(Animation.TYPE_VALUE)
animation.track_set_path(0, "Sprite:transform/pos")
animation.track_insert_key(0, 0.0, Vector2(0, 0))
animation.track_insert_key(0, 1.0, Vector2(100, 100))
$AnimationPlayer.add_animation("move_animation", animation)
```

In this example, a simple movement animation is created for a sprite, moving it from one position to another.

For sprite animations, Godot's AnimatedSprite node is specifically designed to handle frame-by-frame animations. This is particularly useful for characters or objects with complex animations that require a series of images to display their motion.

Creating effective animations often involves understanding the principles of animation, such as timing, anticipation, and exaggeration. These principles help in making animations feel more natural and lively.

Particle systems are another powerful feature in Godot for creating visual effects. The Particles2D node can be used to create a variety of effects, such as smoke, fire, rain, or magical effects. Godot's particle system is highly customizable, allowing for control over aspects like emission shape, velocity, color, and lifetime of particles.

```
# Example: Creating a simple particle system
var particles = Particles2D.new()
```

```
particles.emitting = true
particles.amount = 100
particles.lifetime = 1.0
particles.speed_scale = 20
add_child(particles)
```

In this example, a basic particle system is created, emitting a number of particles over a set lifetime.

Tweening is another animation technique available in Godot. The Tween node can interpolate between values over a specified duration. This is useful for smooth transitions and animations that are not easily achieved with keyframes.

Visual effects in 2D games can also include screen shaders and post-processing effects. Godot supports custom shaders written in its own shading language, similar to GLSL. These can be used to create various visual effects, such as water reflections, glowing effects, or color adjustments.

Layering and ordering of sprites and nodes play a significant role in the overall look of the animation. Properly layering elements can create a sense of depth and focus in your scenes.

Animation blending is a technique to smoothly transition between different animations. This can be especially useful in character animations, where you might need to blend from a walking animation to a running animation seamlessly.

Creating a good animation workflow is important for efficiency, especially when dealing with a large number of animations. This can include organizing your assets, creating reusable animation clips, and setting up an efficient pipeline for integrating animations into your game.

Sound effects synchronized with animations can greatly enhance the impact and feel of the animation. Timing sound effects with key moments in the animation can make actions more impactful and engaging.

In Godot, you can also script animations, providing dynamic control over animation states and transitions based on game logic. This is done using GDScript and can offer a more flexible approach to animation control.

For UI animations, subtle effects like button bounces, fades, or transitions can make the interface more interactive and lively. Godot's UI nodes can be animated just like any other node, allowing for integrated UI animations within your game.

Performance considerations are important when implementing animations and effects, especially for games targeting lower-end devices or mobile platforms. Optimizing your animations and effects to run smoothly without consuming too many resources is crucial.

In conclusion, animations and effects are vital components of 2D game development in Godot. They bring games to life, adding character and depth to the gameplay experience. By leveraging Godot's robust animation tools and understanding key animation principles, developers can create captivating and dynamic 2D games.

3.3 Physics and Collisions in 2D Spaces

Physics and collisions are essential elements in many 2D games, contributing to realism and interactivity. Godot provides a comprehensive set of tools and nodes to handle physics and collision detection efficiently.

In Godot, the `Physics2DServer` is responsible for managing all 2D physics calculations. This includes handling the movement of physical objects, detecting collisions, and applying forces.

The most basic type of physics body in Godot is the `RigidBody2D`. It simulates physics-based movement, responding to forces, torques, and collisions.

3.4 Designing

3.5 Case Study: Developing a Simple 2D Platformer

In this section, we explore the development of a simple 2D platformer game using Godot. This case study will highlight key elements such as character movement, level design, and basic game mechanics.

Setting Up the Project

The first step in developing a 2D platformer in Godot is to set up a new project. After launching Godot, you can create a new project and select a 2D renderer, which is the default setting.

Creating the Player Character

The player character is a central element of any platformer game. Start by creating a new scene and adding a `KinematicBody2D` node. This node is ideal for characters in platformer games due to its ability to handle complex movements and collisions.

```
# Player script (simplified)
extends KinematicBody2D

var velocity = Vector2()
var speed = 200
var jump_force = -400
var gravity = 20

func _physics_process(delta):
    velocity.x = speed * Input.get_action_strength("move_right") - speed * In
put.get_action_strength("move_left")
    velocity.y += gravity
```

```
if Input.is_action_just_pressed("jump") and is_on_floor():
    velocity.y = jump_force

velocity = move_and_slide(velocity, Vector2.UP)
```

This script allows the player to move left and right and jump, using Godot's input actions.

Designing the Level

The next step is designing the level.

Chapter 4: 3D Game Development

4.1 Introduction to 3D in Godot

3D game development in Godot offers a world of possibilities for creating immersive environments, detailed characters, and dynamic gameplay. Godot's powerful 3D engine is capable of handling everything from simple models to complex scenes with advanced lighting and effects.

Understanding the 3D Workspace

When you start a new 3D project in Godot, you'll be presented with the 3D workspace. This is where you'll spend most of your time building and testing your 3D game. The workspace consists of the viewport, where you can view and interact with your 3D scene, and various panels and editors for managing assets and properties.

The Basics of 3D Nodes

In 3D development, nodes are still the fundamental building blocks. Key 3D nodes in Godot include Spatial, which is the base node for all 3D elements, MeshInstance for 3D models, Camera for viewing the scene, and Light nodes for illumination.

Importing 3D Models

Godot supports various 3D model formats, such as OBJ, DAE, and GLTF. Importing models is as simple as dragging and dropping them into the project folder. Once imported, you can add these models to your scene by creating MeshInstance nodes.

Working with Cameras

The Camera node in Godot is essential for viewing your 3D world. Understanding camera properties like FOV (Field of View), depth of field, and frustum is crucial for setting up your scene correctly.

```
# Setting up a camera programmatically
var camera = Camera.new()
camera.fov = 70
camera.near = 0.1
camera.far = 100.0
add_child(camera)
```

This script creates a new camera with specified properties and adds it to the scene.

Lighting

4.3 3D Animations and Rigging

3D animations and rigging are crucial for bringing characters and objects to life in a 3D game environment. Godot provides a range of tools and features to create and implement animations effectively.

Understanding 3D Animation in Godot

3D animation in Godot involves moving, rotating, and scaling 3D models over time. This can be done using keyframe animation, where you set specific values at certain points in time, and Godot interpolates the values in between.

Rigging 3D Models

Rigging is the process of creating a skeleton (or armature) for a 3D model so that it can be animated. This skeleton consists of bones that are used to deform the model in a realistic way.

In Godot, you typically rig your models in a 3D modeling software like Blender, and then import the rigged model into Godot.

Using the AnimationPlayer Node

The `AnimationPlayer` node is a powerful tool in Godot for creating and playing animations. It allows you to create complex animations by keyframing the properties of bones and other objects.

```
# Example: Playing an animation
$AnimationPlayer.play("walk_animation")
```

This script plays a walk animation using the AnimationPlayer node.

Skeletal Animation

Skeletal animation involves animating the bones of a rigged model. This type of animation is efficient and realistic, making it ideal for character animations.

Blend Shapes for Facial Animation

Blend shapes (or morph targets) are used for facial animations and other complex deformations. They work by blending between different shapes of a model.

Creating Animation Trees

For complex characters, Godot's `AnimationTree` node can be used to blend and transition between different animations smoothly, like walking, running, and jumping.

Inverse Kinematics (IK)

Inverse kinematics is a technique used to animate limbs and other parts of a character more naturally. In Godot, IK can be set up in the 3D modeling software or scripted using GDScript for dynamic adjustments.

Importing Animations

Animations created in external software can be imported into Godot along with the 3D models. Godot supports importing animations in various formats like GLTF or DAE.

Animation Loops

Looping animations, such as a character idle or a spinning object, can be set in the AnimationPlayer node. Looping is essential for continuous actions.

Handling Animation Events

Animations can trigger events at specific points, such as sound effects or interactions. This can be handled through the AnimationPlayer's signals or by checking the animation's progress in GDScript.

Layering Animations

Layering multiple animations allows for more complex movements. For example, a character can play a running animation with an upper-body shooting animation.

Physics-based Animation

For more dynamic and responsive animations, physics-based techniques like ragdoll can be implemented. This involves simulating physics on the character's bones.

Animating Non-character Objects

Animations in Godot are not limited to characters.

4.4 Implementing 3D Physics and Collisions

In Godot, implementing 3D physics and collisions is essential for creating realistic interactions and movements within a 3D game environment. This section covers the basics of setting up and working with 3D physics in Godot.

Understanding 3D Physics Bodies

Godot offers several types of physics bodies for 3D, each serving different purposes. `RigidBody`, `StaticBody`, and `KinematicBody` are the primary types used in 3D physics simulations.

RigidBody in 3D

RigidBody in 3D is used for objects that need to react to forces, torque, and collisions in a realistic manner. This body type is governed by the physics engine and is ideal for dynamic objects in your game.

```
# Example: Creating a RigidBody in GDScript
var rigid_body = RigidBody.new()
add_child(rigid_body)
```

This script adds a RigidBody to your scene, allowing it to interact physically with other objects.

StaticBody for Fixed Objects

StaticBody is used for non-movable objects that can interact with other physics bodies. It's perfect for creating floors, walls, and other static elements in your 3D world.

KinematicBody for Controlled Movements

KinematicBody is used for objects that require precise control over their movement. Unlike RigidBody, KinematicBody does not respond to physics forces but can still interact with other physics bodies.

Setting Up Collision Shapes

Collision shapes define the physical shape of your physics bodies for collision detection. In Godot, CollisionShape or CollisionPolygon nodes are used alongside your physics bodies.

```
# Example: Adding a collision shape to a RigidBody
var collision_shape = CollisionShape.new()
collision_shape.shape = BoxShape.new()
collision_shape.shape.extents = Vector3(1, 1, 1)
rigid_body.add_child(collision_shape)
```

In this example, a box-shaped collision shape is added to a RigidBody.

Physics Materials

Physics materials in Godot allow you to define properties like friction and bounce for physics bodies. These materials are applied to collision shapes to affect how they interact with other objects.

Simulating Gravity and Forces

In 3D physics, simulating gravity and applying forces is crucial for realistic movement. Godot allows you to set global gravity settings and apply forces to individual physics bodies.

Handling Collisions

Detecting and responding to collisions is a key part of 3D physics. This can be done by connecting to signals emitted by physics bodies or by checking collision information during the physics process.

Implementing Raycasting

Raycasting is used to detect objects in a line from a certain point in space. This is useful for line-of-sight calculations, shooting mechanics, or detecting objects in front of the player.

Physics Layers and Masks

Layers and masks determine which physics bodies can interact with each other. By setting these properties, you can control the interaction between different objects in your game.

Joints and Constraints

For more complex physics simulations, Godot offers various types of joints and constraints. These can be used to connect physics bodies in specific ways, like hinges, sliders, or springs.

Creating Vehicles

Godot's `VehicleBody` and `VehicleWheel` nodes can be used to simulate car-like vehicles. These nodes provide properties and methods for creating and controlling vehicles in your game.

Integrating Animation with Physics

Combining physics with animation can create more dynamic and responsive character movements. For instance, using physics for ragdoll effects or blending animations based on physics interactions.

Optimizing Physics Performance

3D physics can be performance-intensive. Optimizing your physics setup is crucial, especially for complex scenes or mobile platforms. This includes simplifying collision shapes, reducing the number of physics bodies, and tweaking physics settings.

Debugging Physics

Debugging physics issues can be challenging. Godot provides tools like the Visible Collision Shapes option and the Physics Debugger to help visualize and diagnose physics-related problems.

Conclusion

Implementing 3D physics and collisions in Godot is essential for creating interactive and realistic 3D environments. By understanding the different physics bodies, setting up collision shapes, and utilizing the physics engine's capabilities, you can add an extra layer of realism and immersion to your 3D games.

4.5 Creating Immersive 3D Environments

Creating immersive 3D environments in Godot is key to engaging players and enhancing the overall gaming experience. This involves a combination of various elements such as terrain, environmental effects, lighting, and sound.

Designing the Terrain

The foundation of any 3D environment is its terrain. In Godot, terrains can be created using the GridMap node or by importing models from external 3D modeling software.

Chapter 5: Scripting and Programming

5.1 Deep Dive into GDScript

GDScript is Godot's native scripting language, designed specifically for high-level game development. It offers a balance of performance and ease of use, making it an ideal choice for both beginners and experienced developers.

Understanding GDScript Basics

GDScript is a dynamically typed language, heavily inspired by Python. Its syntax is clean and easy to read, which makes it accessible for those new to programming.

```
# Basic GDScript Syntax
var health = 100
if health > 0:
    print("Player is alive")
```

This example shows variable declaration and a simple if statement in GDScript.

Variables and Data Types

GDScript supports various data types including integers, floats, strings, arrays, and dictionaries. Understanding these types is essential for effective scripting.

```
# Different data types in GDScript
var name = "Godot"   # String
var score = 10       # Integer
var health = 95.5    # Float
var items = ["sword", "shield", "potion"]  # Array
var player = {"name": "Hero", "class": "Warrior"}  # Dictionary
```

Functions in GDScript

Functions are reusable blocks of code. They are used to execute specific tasks and can return values.

```
func add_numbers(a, b):
    return a + b
```

This function, add_numbers, takes two parameters and returns their sum.

Control Flow Statements

Control flow statements, such as if-else conditions and loops, control the execution of code blocks in GDScript.

```
# Using an if-else statement
if score > 50:
    print("
```

5.3 Effective Debugging and Error Handling

Effective debugging and error handling are critical components of game development in Godot. Understanding how to identify, diagnose, and resolve issues is key to creating stable and reliable games.

Understanding Godot's Debugger

Godot's built-in debugger is a powerful tool for diagnosing and fixing issues in your game. It allows you to pause execution, step through code, inspect variables, and view error messages.

Using Breakpoints

Breakpoints are an essential debugging feature.

5.4 Optimization Techniques for Game Scripts

Optimizing game scripts is crucial for improving performance and ensuring a smooth gameplay experience. In Godot, there are several techniques and best practices for optimizing GDScript and C# scripts.

Understanding Script Performance

Performance in scripting largely revolves around how quickly and efficiently scripts are executed. Factors such as algorithm complexity, loop efficiency, and resource usage play significant roles.

Profiling Scripts

Use Godot's built-in profiler to identify performance bottlenecks in your scripts. Look for functions or areas in your code that take up a lot of processing time.

Efficient Use of Data Structures

Choosing the right data structure can significantly impact performance. For instance, using Dictionaries for quick lookups or Arrays for ordered data can optimize your script's efficiency.

Reducing Function Calls

Minimizing the number of function calls, especially in frequently executed code such as _process or _physics_process, can improve performance.

```
# Optimize by reducing unnecessary function calls
func _process(delta):
    # Avoid putting heavy function calls here
```

Optimizing Loops

Loops, especially nested loops, can be performance-intensive. Optimize loops by reducing their complexity and exiting early when possible.

Caching Frequently Used Values

Caching values that don't change often, instead of recalculating them each time, can save processing time.

```
# Caching an often-used value
var cached_value = calculate_expensive_value()
```

Lazy Loading of Resources

Load resources on demand (lazy loading) rather than all at once at the start. This can reduce initial load times and spread resource loading over time.

Using Signals Wisely

While signals are powerful, overusing them or connecting too many can impact performance. Use signals judiciously.

Memory Management

Be mindful of memory usage. Avoid unnecessary allocations and free up resources when they're no longer needed.

Writing Efficient Conditional Statements

Optimize conditional statements by placing the most likely or quickest conditions first.

```
# Efficient conditional checks
if simple_condition and complex_condition:
    # Do something
```

Vector and Mathematical Calculations

Optimize vector and mathematical calculations by simplifying expressions and avoiding redundant calculations.

Multithreading for Heavy Tasks

Consider using multithreading for resource-intensive tasks. However, be aware of the complexities and potential issues like race conditions.

Debouncing and Throttling

Implement debouncing or throttling for input handling or functions that don't need to run every frame.

Avoiding Global Variables

Limit the use of global variables. Accessing global variables can be slower and they can also lead to harder-to-maintain code.

Script Compilation and Parsing

In C#, be aware of the cost of compilation and parsing. Precompiling scripts and avoiding runtime evaluations can improve performance.

Using GDNative for Critical Sections

For extremely performance-critical sections, consider using GDNative extensions, which allow you to write performance-critical code in languages like C++.

Regular Testing and Optimization

Regularly test your game's performance and optimize as needed. What works well in the early stages of development might not hold up as your game grows.

Conclusion

Script optimization is an ongoing process in game development. By employing these techniques and regularly profiling your game, you can significantly improve performance and create a smoother experience for players.

5.5 Integrating External Libraries and APIs

Integrating external libraries and APIs into your Godot projects can significantly expand the functionality and capabilities of your games. This section explores the process and considerations involved in integrating third-party tools with Godot.

Understanding Godot's Extensibility

Godot is designed to be extensible, allowing developers to integrate external libraries and APIs. This includes everything from physics engines to social media APIs.

Choosing Appropriate Libraries

Select libraries that are compatible with Godot and fit the needs of your project. Consider factors like licensing, platform support, and community backing.

GDNative for Custom Integrations

GDNative is Godot's system for integrating native code written in C, C++, or other languages. It's particularly useful for performance-critical operations or interfacing with low-level APIs.

Setting Up GDNative

Setting up GDNative involves creating a native script, compiling it for your target platforms, and linking it to your Godot project.

```
# Example of using a GDNative script
var gdnative_script = preload("res://path/to/gdnative_script.gdns")
var native_node = gdnative_script.new()
```

Interfacing with Web APIs

For web APIs, you can use Godot's HTTPRequest node to send and receive HTTP requests. This is useful for features like online leaderboards or content updates.

```
# Sending an HTTP request
var http_request = HTTPRequest.new()
add_child(http_request)
http_request.request("https://api.example.com/data")
```

Working with Mobile APIs

For mobile-specific features like in-app purchases or advertisements, you can use Godot's mobile platform modules or third-party plugins.

Integrating Social Media

Integrating social media platforms can involve using web APIs or specialized SDKs. This can enable features like sharing game achievements or multiplayer interactions.

Utilizing Physics and AI Libraries

External physics and AI libraries can provide advanced functionalities beyond Godot's built-in features. Ensure they are compatible with Godot's rendering and physics systems.

Handling Dependencies

Manage dependencies carefully to ensure compatibility and ease of updates. Consider using package managers or Godot's asset library.

Security Considerations

When integrating external APIs, especially for online interactions, prioritize security. This includes using encryption for data transmission and safeguarding API keys.

Dealing with Platform-Specific Libraries

Some libraries are platform-specific. Ensure that you have platform-specific code paths in your game to handle these cases.

Custom Plugins for Editor Functionality

Create custom plugins for the Godot editor if you need to extend its functionality or integrate external tools into the development workflow.

Documentation and Support

Good documentation is crucial for working with external libraries. Additionally, consider the level of support and community around the library.

Performance Impact

Assess the performance impact of external libraries. They should not significantly degrade the performance of your game.

Legal and Licensing Issues

Understand the legal and licensing implications of using external libraries. Ensure compliance with the licenses of the libraries you use.

Testing and Debugging

Thoroughly test the integration to ensure stability and compatibility. Debugging issues with external libraries can be challenging, so robust testing is essential.

Keeping Libraries Updated

Keep your external libraries updated to benefit from bug fixes, security patches, and new features.

Conclusion

Integrating external libraries and APIs can significantly enhance the functionality of your Godot games. Careful selection, integration, and management of these external resources are key to successfully expanding your game's capabilities.

6.2 Implementing Background Music and Sound Effects

In this section, we'll delve deeper into the implementation of background music and sound effects in Godot. Building upon the basics covered in the previous section, we'll explore more advanced techniques to enhance your game's audio experience.

Crossfading Background Music

Crossfading is a technique that allows for smooth transitions between different background music tracks. For instance, when moving from one game level to another, you might want to fade out the current background music and fade in a new track. Here's an example of how you can achieve crossfading in Godot:

```
extends Node

var current_bg_music: AudioStreamPlayer
var next_bg_music: AudioStreamPlayer

func _ready():
    current_bg_music = AudioStreamPlayer.new()
    next_bg_music = AudioStreamPlayer.new()

    current_bg_music.stream = load("res://current_bg_music.ogg")
    next_bg_music.stream = load("res://next_bg_music.ogg")

    add_child(current_bg_music)
    add_child(next_bg_music)

    current_bg_music.play()

func fade_and_switch_music():
    current_bg_music.fadeout(2.0)   # Fade out over 2 seconds
    next_bg_music.play()
}
```

In this code, we have two AudioStreamPlayer nodes: current_bg_music and next_bg_music. When it's time to switch the background music, you call the fade_and_switch_music() function. This function fades out the current background music over 2 seconds and then starts playing the new background music.

Randomizing Sound Effects

To make your game's audio more dynamic and less predictable, you can introduce randomness when playing sound effects. For example, if you have multiple explosion sound effects, you can play a different one each time. Here's a basic example:

```
extends Node

var explosion_sounds: Array = []

func _ready():
    for i in range(1, 4):  # Assuming you have explosion1.wav, explosion2.wav
, explosion3.wav
        var sound_effect = AudioStreamPlayer.new()
        sound_effect.stream = load("res://explosion" + str(i) + ".wav")
        add_child(sound_effect)
        explosion_sounds.append(sound_effect)

func play_random_explosion():
    var random_index = randi() % explosion_sounds.size()
    explosion_sounds[random_index].play()
}
```

In this code, we load multiple explosion sound effects and store them in an array. When you call play_random_explosion(), it selects a random explosion sound effect from the array and plays it. This adds variety to the game's audio.

Spatial Audio

Godot supports spatial audio, which simulates sound coming from specific locations in the game world. This can enhance the immersion and realism of your game. To use spatial audio, you can attach an AudioStreamPlayer2D or AudioStreamPlayer3D node to your in-game objects.

```
extends Area2D

var audio_player: AudioStreamPlayer2D

func _ready():
    audio_player = AudioStreamPlayer2D.new()
    audio_player.stream = load("res://footstep.wav")
    add_child(audio_player)

func play_footstep_sound():
    audio_player.play()
}
```

In this example, we create an AudioStreamPlayer2D node attached to a 2D area. When you call play_footstep_sound(), it plays the footstep sound effect from the position of the 2D area.

6.3 Dynamic Audio: Adjusting Sounds Based on Gameplay

In this section, we'll explore the concept of dynamic audio in game development using Godot. Dynamic audio involves adjusting sound elements in real-time based on gameplay events, creating a more immersive and responsive experience for players. Here, we'll discuss various techniques to achieve dynamic audio in your Godot games.

Audio Panning

Audio panning is the technique of adjusting the balance of sound between the left and right audio channels to simulate the direction from which a sound originates. This adds a spatial dimension to your game's audio, making it more realistic. In Godot, you can achieve audio panning by manipulating the pan property of audio players.

Here's a basic example of audio panning:

```
extends Node2D

var audio_player: AudioStreamPlayer2D
var listener_position: Vector2

func _ready():
```

```
    audio_player = AudioStreamPlayer2D.new()
    audio_player.stream = load("res://enemy_alert.wav")
    add_child(audio_player)

func update_audio_panning(enemy_position: Vector2):
    var distance = listener_position.distance_to(enemy_position)
    var pan = (enemy_position.x - listener_position.x) / distance
    audio_player.pan = pan
    audio_player.play()
}
```

In this code, we have an `AudioStreamPlayer2D` attached to a 2D object. The `update_audio_panning()` function calculates the pan value based on the position of an enemy relative to the listener (e.g., the player). Adjusting the pan property dynamically changes the perceived direction of the sound.

Volume Modulation

Volume modulation involves dynamically changing the volume of audio sources to create variations in sound intensity. This technique is often used to add realism to effects like footsteps, gunfire, or environmental sounds. In Godot, you can achieve volume modulation by altering the `volume_db` property of audio players.

Here's a simple example of volume modulation for footsteps:

```
extends Node2D

var audio_player: AudioStreamPlayer2D

func _ready():
    audio_player = AudioStreamPlayer2D.new()
    audio_player.stream = load("res://footstep.wav")
    add_child(audio_player)

func play_footstep(volume_modifier: float):
    audio_player.volume_db = -10 + (volume_modifier * 10)   # Adjust as needed
    audio_player.play()
}
```

In this code, the `play_footstep()` function takes a `volume_modifier` parameter, which can be used to control the volume of the footstep sound.

6.4 Working with Audio Streams and Players

In this section, we'll delve into more advanced aspects of audio management in Godot, focusing on working with audio streams and players. Audio streams and players give you fine-grained control over audio playback, making it possible to create intricate audio systems for your games.

Audio Streams vs. Audio Players

Before we dive into the details, let's clarify the distinction between audio streams and audio players in Godot.

- **Audio Streams:** Audio streams are resources that represent audio data. They can be loaded from audio files or generated programmatically. Audio streams don't directly play sound but serve as the source of audio data. Examples of audio stream types in Godot include `AudioStream`, `AudioStreamSample`, and `AudioStreamGenerator`.

- **Audio Players:** Audio players are nodes that handle the playback of audio streams. They can be attached to objects in your game world and are responsible for playing, pausing, stopping, and controlling the audio. Examples of audio player nodes in Godot include `AudioStreamPlayer`, `AudioStreamPlayer2D`, and `AudioStreamPlayer3D`.

Custom Audio Streams

In some cases, you might need to generate audio programmatically or manipulate existing audio data before playing it.

6.5 Advanced Audio Techniques for Immersive Experiences

In this section, we will explore advanced audio techniques that can be used in Godot to create immersive and engaging audio experiences in your games. These techniques go beyond the basics of audio playback and provide more depth and realism to your game's audio.

Audio Occlusion and Spatial Awareness

Audio occlusion is the simulation of sound obstruction by objects in the game world. It adds realism by making sounds muffled or less audible when they are blocked by obstacles. To implement audio occlusion in Godot, you can use the `AudioServer`'s `ray_pick` method to check for obstacles between the audio source and the listener.

Chapter 7:

7.2 Creating Heads-Up Displays (HUDs)

In this section, we will explore the creation of Heads-Up Displays (HUDs) in Godot. HUDs are essential for displaying critical information and elements directly on the game screen, such as health bars, score counters, minimaps, and more. Designing effective HUDs can significantly enhance the player's experience by providing them with important real-time feedback.

The Role of HUDs in Game Design

HUDs serve multiple purposes in game design:

1. **Information Presentation:** HUDs convey vital game information, such as character health, ammunition, objective progress, and minimap details, to players in real-time.

2. **Immersion:** Well-designed HUDs blend seamlessly with the game world, enhancing immersion by providing information in a contextually relevant manner.

3. **Feedback:** HUDs offer immediate feedback to players about the consequences of their actions, making the gameplay experience more engaging.

4. **Navigation:** HUD elements like minimaps and waypoints help players navigate complex game environments.

Creating HUD Elements

Godot provides various nodes and techniques for creating HUD elements:

CanvasLayer: HUDs are often created using CanvasLayer nodes. These nodes are drawn on top of the game world and remain fixed in screen space.

7.3 Responsive UIs for Multiple Screen Sizes

Creating responsive user interfaces (UIs) is crucial in modern game development, as players use a variety of devices with different screen sizes and resolutions. In this section, we'll explore how to design UIs in Godot that adapt gracefully to various screen sizes, ensuring that your game looks and functions well on a wide range of platforms.

The Challenge of Multiple Screen Sizes

Games can be played on devices with vastly different screen sizes, from large desktop monitors to small mobile phones and everything in between. Ensuring that your UI remains readable and usable on all these devices is a significant challenge.

Responsive UI design addresses this challenge by creating layouts and assets that can adapt to different screen dimensions. The goal is to maintain a consistent user experience regardless of the device being used.

Use Containers for Layout

Godot provides container nodes such as VBoxContainer, HBoxContainer, and GridContainer that make it easier to create responsive UI layouts. These containers automatically arrange child nodes, adjusting their positions and sizes to fit the available space.

For example, you can use a VBoxContainer to stack UI elements vertically, ensuring they maintain their relative positions on different screen sizes. Here's a simplified example:

```
extends Control

func _ready():
    var vbox = VBoxContainer.new()
```

```
add_child(vbox)

var label1 = Label.new()
label1.text = "Option 1"
vbox.add_child(label1)

var label2 = Label.new()
label2.text = "Option 2"
vbox.add_child(label2)

var label3 = Label.new()
label3.text = "Option 3"
vbox.add_child(label3)

vbox.rect_min_size = Vector2(200, 300)
```

In this example, we create a VBoxContainer and add three Label nodes to it. The VBoxContainer automatically arranges the labels vertically. By setting the rect_min_size property of the container, you can specify a minimum size for the container, ensuring that it doesn't shrink too small on smaller screens.

Use Anchors and Expanding Containers

Anchors and expanding containers help elements maintain their positions relative to the screen edges or other UI elements. This is particularly useful when designing UIs that need to adapt to various screen sizes.

Godot's anchor system allows you to attach UI elements to the sides of the screen or other UI elements. For example, you can anchor a button to the top-right corner of the screen so that it remains there regardless of the screen size.

```
# Anchor a button to the top-right corner of the screen
var button = $Button
button.rect_min_size = Vector2(100, 50)
button.rect_min_size_authorized = true  # Enable minimum size control

button.anchor_right = 1.0  # Anchor to the right edge of the parent container
(1.0 means 100%)
button.anchor_top = 0.0    # Anchor to the top edge of the parent container (
0.0 means 0%)
```

In this example, we anchor a button to the top-right corner of its parent container. The rect_min_size properties ensure that the button maintains a minimum size, and rect_min_size_authorized allows the button to control its minimum size.

Test on Different Devices

Testing your responsive UI on various devices and screen resolutions is essential to ensure that it works as intended. Use Godot's built-in viewport scaling options and preview your game on different screen sizes to identify and address any layout issues.

Dynamic UI Elements

Consider using dynamic UI elements that can adjust their content based on screen size. For example, if you have a list of items in your UI, you can show more items on larger screens and fewer on smaller screens.

Responsive UI design is essential for providing a consistent and enjoyable experience to players on different devices. By using containers, anchors, expanding containers, and testing on various devices, you can create UIs that adapt seamlessly to different screen sizes, ensuring that your game remains accessible and visually appealing to a wide audience.

7.4 Animating UI Elements for Enhanced

7.5 Scripting for Interactive UI Elements

Scripting plays a crucial role in making UI elements in your Godot game interactive and responsive to player actions. In this section, we'll explore how to use scripting to add functionality and behavior to your UI elements, enabling them to perform actions, respond to events, and enhance the overall user experience.

Event Handling

To make your UI elements interactive, you need to handle user events like button clicks, mouse movements, and keyboard input. In Godot, this is typically done by connecting signals emitted by UI elements to functions in your scripts.

For example, you can connect a button's pressed signal to a function that performs a specific action when the button is clicked:

```
func _ready():
    var button = $Button
    button.connect("pressed", self, "_on_button_pressed")

func _on_button_pressed():
    # Perform the desired action when the button is pressed
    pass
```

In this code, we connect the pressed signal of a button to the _on_button_pressed function. When the button is pressed, the connected function is executed.

Changing UI Element Properties

8.2 Implementing 2D and 3D Collisions

Collisions are a fundamental aspect of game physics, and Godot provides robust support for handling 2D and 3D collisions. In this section, we'll explore how to implement collisions in both 2D and 3D game environments using Godot's physics engine.

2D Collisions

Godot's 2D physics engine is designed for 2D games and offers features like rigid bodies, shapes, and collision layers. To implement 2D collisions, follow these steps:

1. **Create Rigid Bodies:** Design your game objects as 2D rigid bodies. Attach collision shapes (e.g., RectangleShape2D, CircleShape2D) to these rigid bodies to define their collision boundaries.

2. **Set Collision Layers and Masks:** In the Inspector panel, configure the collision layers and masks for each 2D rigid body. Collision layers determine which layers an object belongs to, and masks define which layers it can collide with. This allows you to control collision interactions.

3. **Handling Collisions:** Implement collision callbacks by connecting signals such as body_entered and body_exited to functions in your scripts. These functions will be called when objects enter or exit collision with the 2D rigid body.

```
func _on_body_entered(body):
    if body is KinematicBody2D:
        # Handle collision with a specific type of object (KinematicBody2D)
        pass
```

Collision Layers in Code:

8.3 Simulating Realistic Movements and Behaviors

Realistic movements and behaviors of objects in a game are crucial for creating an immersive and engaging player experience. In this section, we'll explore how to simulate realistic movements and behaviors using Godot's physics engine and scripting capabilities.

Simulating Gravity

Gravity is a fundamental force in the physical world, and simulating it is essential for creating realistic movements in your game. In Godot, you can easily apply gravity to objects using the gravity_scale property of rigid bodies.

```
# Enable gravity for a rigid body
rigid_body.gravity_scale = 1.0
```

By setting the gravity_scale to a positive value, you can simulate the effect of gravity pulling objects downward. Adjust the value to control the strength of gravity for different objects.

Applying Forces and Impulses

To create realistic movements and behaviors, you can apply forces and impulses to objects in your game. Forces simulate continuous influences like wind or thrust, while impulses represent sudden impacts. These actions can be applied to both 2D and 3D rigid bodies.

```
# Apply a force to a rigid body
var force = Vector3(0, 10, 0)  # Applying an upward force
rigid_body.apply_impulse(Vector3.ZERO, force)
```

In this example, we apply an upward force to a 3D rigid body. The `apply_impulse` function is used to apply the force at a specific point on the object.

Constraints and Joints

Godot provides various constraints and joints that allow you to simulate complex behaviors and interactions between objects. These include:

- **HingeJoint:** Simulates a hinge-like connection between two objects, allowing them to rotate around a common axis.

- **SliderJoint:** Enables sliding movement between two objects along a specified axis, similar to a drawer or slider mechanism.

- **SpringArm:** Creates spring-like behavior, allowing objects to stretch and compress while following a target.

- **DampedSpring:** Similar to SpringArm but with dampening for smoother motion.

- **PulleyJoint:** Simulates a pulley system where objects can be connected and moved using ropes or cables.

By using these constraints and joints, you can simulate realistic mechanical interactions, vehicle suspensions, and complex physical behaviors in your game.

Ragdoll Physics

Ragdoll physics is a technique used to simulate the movement of characters or objects with multiple interconnected rigid bodies. This approach is commonly used for characters to create realistic reactions to impacts, falls, or explosions. Godot provides tools and functions to set up ragdoll physics in your game, allowing you to control the behavior of individual body parts.

Raycasting

Raycasting is a technique for simulating interactions between objects and detecting collisions along a specific path or direction. It is often used for tasks like character movement, weapon aiming, and object interactions. In Godot, you can perform raycasting using the `ray-cast` functions available for both 2D and 3D physics.

```
# Perform a raycast in 3D
var result = rigid_body.ray_cast(ray_start, ray_end)
if result.has_hit():
    var hit_position = result.to
    var hit_normal = result.normal
    # Handle the collision or interaction
```

Raycasting allows you to determine whether a ray intersects with objects in the game world and gather information about the point of intersection and surface normal.

Steering and Pathfinding

For simulating realistic movement and behavior in characters or vehicles, you can implement steering behaviors and pathfinding algorithms. Steering behaviors help objects navigate the environment intelligently, while pathfinding algorithms like A* assist in finding optimal paths around obstacles.

Godot provides navigation and pathfinding tools to simplify the implementation of steering and pathfinding behaviors in your game. These tools allow characters and objects to move efficiently, avoid obstacles, and reach their destinations while considering realistic movements and behaviors.

In conclusion, simulating realistic movements and behaviors is essential for creating immersive and engaging gameplay experiences in your Godot game. By applying gravity, using forces and impulses, employing constraints and joints, implementing ragdoll physics, using raycasting, and incorporating steering and pathfinding, you can create dynamic and lifelike interactions between objects, characters, and the game environment. Understanding these techniques and principles will help you achieve a higher level of realism and player engagement in your game.

8.4 Working with Particles and Environmental Effects

Particles and environmental effects play a significant role in enhancing the visual appeal and immersion of your game. Godot provides a versatile and powerful particle system that allows you to create various effects, such as fire, smoke, rain, explosions, and more. In this section, we'll explore how to work with particles and environmental effects in your Godot project.

Particle System Overview

Godot's particle system is a node-based system that allows you to emit and control a large number of particles in real-time. The key components of the particle system include:

- **Particles2D and Particles3D Nodes:** These nodes represent 2D and 3D particle systems, respectively, and serve as containers for emitting and controlling particles.

Particle Texture:

8.5 Advanced Physics Simulations for Realistic Gameplay

Advanced physics simulations are often required to achieve realistic and immersive gameplay experiences in Godot. In this section, we'll delve into more sophisticated aspects of Godot's physics engine and techniques to enhance the realism of your game.

Soft Body Physics

Soft body physics simulate deformable and flexible objects, such as cloth, rubber, or jelly-like materials. While Godot's built-in physics engine primarily handles rigid body simulations, you can achieve soft body effects using custom scripts and physics techniques.

To implement soft body physics:

1. **Mesh Deformation:** Create a 3D mesh representing the soft body object, such as cloth. Use the MeshInstance node to add the mesh to your scene.

Physics Integration: Write custom scripts to control the physics behavior of the soft body.

9.2 Creating Multiplayer Games: Client-Server Model

Creating multiplayer games often involves implementing a client-server model, where a dedicated server manages the game world and communicates with multiple clients. In this section, we'll dive into the details of setting up a multiplayer game using the client-server model in Godot.

Server Configuration

In the client-server model, the server acts as the authoritative source of truth for the game state. It simulates the game world, processes player actions, and sends updates to clients. To set up the server in Godot:

1. **Create a Dedicated Server Scene:** Start by creating a new scene dedicated to the server. This scene will contain the game logic and handle client connections.

Add a NetworkedMultiplayerENet Node: In the server scene, add a NetworkedMultiplayerENet node and configure it as the server.

9.3 Handling Latency and Synchronization Issues

Latency and synchronization issues are common challenges in multiplayer game development. Players may experience delays in receiving updates from the server, leading to a less responsive and enjoyable gameplay experience. In this section, we'll explore techniques and strategies to address these issues in Godot-based multiplayer games.

Understanding Latency

Latency, often referred to as "ping" or "lag," is the delay between a player's action and the corresponding result in the game. High latency can lead to various issues, including delayed character movements, incorrect hit detection, and synchronization problems.

There are two primary sources of latency in multiplayer games:

1. **Network Latency:** This is the time it takes for data to travel between the player's device and the server or other players' devices. Network latency is influenced by factors such as distance, network congestion, and the quality of the player's internet connection.

2. **Server Processing Latency:** The server itself introduces latency as it processes incoming data, updates the game state, and sends updates to all connected clients. The efficiency of your server's logic and the complexity of the game state can affect server processing latency.

Predictive Input and Client-Side Prediction

One way to mitigate the effects of latency is to implement predictive input and client-side prediction. With this technique, clients predict the outcome of their own actions based on their local inputs before receiving updates from the server.

For example, if a player presses the "move forward" key, the client immediately moves the player character forward on their screen, even before the server confirms the action. When the server's update arrives, the client reconciles the predicted position with the server's authoritative position. If they match, there's no issue. If they differ, the client smoothly corrects the position to match the server's version.

```
# Client-side prediction for player movement
func _physics_process(delta):
    # Predicted position based on local input
    var predicted_position = position + input_direction * move_speed * delta

    # Apply input locally
    position = predicted_position

    # Send input to the server
    rpc("sync_input", input_direction)

# Server receives input and updates player position
remote func sync_input(input_direction):
    # Validate input and update player position
```

Lag Compensation

Lag compensation techniques aim to make the game feel fair even when players have varying levels of latency. For example, in a first-person shooter, lag compensation can adjust hit detection to account for the delay between a shot being fired and it registering on the target.

Godot provides tools to implement lag compensation, including techniques like extrapolation, interpolation, and rollback. These techniques help ensure that gameplay interactions appear smooth and fair for all players, regardless of their latency.

Networked SceneTree and Remote Instancing

The Networked SceneTree feature in Godot can help address synchronization issues by creating separate game scenes for each player or group of players. Each client has its own SceneTree, which allows for independent updates and interactions.

In addition, Godot offers Remote Instancing, which allows you to create instances of objects on remote peers and keep them synchronized. This feature is useful for games with dynamic and interactive environments where players need to see and interact with objects created by others.

Latency Compensation for Animations and Visual Effects

Latency can also affect the synchronization of animations and visual effects in multiplayer games. To compensate for latency, you can:

- Apply interpolation techniques to smooth out character animations and movements.
- Predict the trajectories of projectiles or objects for smoother visual effects.
- Implement mechanisms for handling delays in visual feedback, such as hit confirmation animations.

In conclusion, handling latency and synchronization issues is essential for creating a responsive and enjoyable multiplayer game experience. Techniques like predictive input, client-side prediction, lag compensation, and the use of Godot's Networked SceneTree and Remote Instancing can help mitigate these challenges. By carefully addressing latency-related issues, you can enhance the fairness and playability of your multiplayer games, providing a better experience for players with varying levels of network latency.

9.4 Implementing Chat and Communication Features

Communication is a vital aspect of multiplayer games, enabling players to interact, strategize, and coordinate with each other. Implementing chat and communication features in Godot-based multiplayer games enhances the player experience and fosters community engagement. In this section, we'll explore how to integrate chat and communication features effectively.

In-game chat allows players to send text messages to each other within the game environment. To implement in-game chat in Godot:

1. **Chat Box UI:** Create a chat box UI element where messages will be displayed. This can be a TextEdit node or a RichTextLabel for more advanced formatting.

2. **Input Field:** Add an input field where players can type and send messages.

3. **Message Sending:** Implement logic to send messages to other players or the server when the player presses the send button or hits the Enter key.

4. **Message Reception:** Receive and display incoming messages from other players or the server in the chat box.

Here's a simplified example of sending and receiving chat messages in Godot:

```
extends Control

# UI elements
var chat_box : RichTextLabel
var input_field : LineEdit

# Handle sending a chat message
func _on_send_button_pressed():
    var message = input_field.text
    if message != "":
        # Send the message to other players or the server
        rpc("send_chat_message", message)
        input_field.text = ""

# Receive and display chat messages
func display_chat_message(sender, message):
    chat_box.bbcode_text += "[color=blue]" + sender + "[/color]: " + message
+ "\n"

# Server receives chat message and broadcasts it to all clients
remote func send_chat_message(message):
    # Validate the message and sender
    # Broadcast the message to all clients
    rpc("display_chat_message", get_peer_username(get_tree().get_rpc_sender()
), message)

# Helper function to get the username of a peer
func get_peer_username(peer_id):
    # Retrieve the username associated with the peer
```

Voice Chat

Voice chat adds another layer of immersion and interaction to multiplayer games. Implementing voice chat requires integrating audio input and output, as well as managing voice communication between players.

To implement voice chat in Godot:

1. **Audio Input:** Capture audio from the player's microphone using the `AudioServer` or a third-party library like WebRTC.

2. **Audio Output:** Play audio received from other players through speakers or headphones.

3. **Networking:** Send audio data as part of the network communication between clients and the server. This may involve using custom network protocols or libraries.

4. **Volume and Quality Control:** Implement controls for adjusting voice chat volume and quality to ensure a good user experience.

5. **Push-to-Talk or Voice Activation:** Allow players to choose between push-to-talk or voice activation modes for transmitting their voice.

6. **Network Optimization:** Optimize audio data transmission to minimize latency and bandwidth usage.

Implementing voice chat can be complex, and you may need to explore third-party libraries or plugins for more advanced voice communication features.

Emotes and Gestures

Emotes and gestures add non-verbal communication to your multiplayer game. Players can express emotions, reactions, and actions through pre-defined or custom emotes and gestures. Implementing emotes and gestures involves:

1. **Emote System:** Create a system for triggering and displaying emotes and gestures. This can be a menu, gesture recognition, or hotkey-based system.

2. **Emote Animations:** Animate player characters or avatars to perform the selected emote or gesture.

3. **Emote Text or Icons:** Display text or icons indicating the selected emote or gesture above the player character or in a chat window.

4. **Networking:** Synchronize emote and gesture actions among all players to ensure everyone sees the same animations and messages.

5. **Custom Emotes:** Allow players to create custom emotes and gestures for personalization.

6. **Moderation:** Implement moderation features to prevent abuse or inappropriate content in emotes and gestures.

In addition to player-to-player communication, multiplayer games often require the ability to broadcast global announcements and system messages. These messages can inform players about important events, updates, or server maintenance.

To implement global announcements and system messages:

1. **Admin Controls:** Create admin controls or server commands for sending global announcements and system messages.

2. **Message Display:** Determine how and where to display these messages, such as in a dedicated chat channel or as pop-up notifications.

3. **Formatting:** Format system messages to distinguish them from player messages, and consider using different colors or styles.

4. **Timestamps:** Add timestamps to messages for reference and clarity.

In conclusion, implementing chat and communication features in Godot-based multiplayer games enhances player interaction and engagement. Whether it's in-game chat, voice chat, emotes and gestures, or global announcements, effective communication features contribute to a more social and immersive multiplayer experience. Careful design and moderation are essential to maintain a positive and enjoyable multiplayer environment.

9.5 Security Considerations in Multiplayer Games

Security is a critical aspect of multiplayer game development to protect both players and the integrity of the gaming experience. In this section, we'll explore important security considerations and best practices when developing multiplayer games in Godot.

Player Authentication

Player authentication is the process of verifying the identity of players before allowing them to access a multiplayer game. Proper authentication helps prevent unauthorized access, cheating, and impersonation.

To implement player authentication in Godot:

Chapter 10: AI and Game Logic

10.1 Implementing AI: Pathfinding and Decision Making

Artificial Intelligence (AI) is a crucial component of many modern games, enhancing the player's experience by providing intelligent, dynamic, and challenging opponents or allies. In this section, we'll delve into the implementation of AI in Godot, focusing on pathfinding and decision-making processes.

The Role of AI in Games

AI in games simulates the behavior of entities, such as characters or enemies, to make them appear intelligent and responsive. Game AI often involves two fundamental aspects:

1. **Pathfinding:** Determining the best route for an entity to reach a specific location, avoiding obstacles and following a path that makes sense within the game world.

2. **Decision Making:** Making choices or decisions based on various factors, such as the entity's goals, the current game state, and its understanding of the environment.

Pathfinding Algorithms

Pathfinding is a critical component of AI for characters or entities that need to navigate game worlds efficiently. Godot provides tools and built-in navigation features that support popular pathfinding algorithms, such as A* (A-star), Dijkstra's, and more.

To implement pathfinding in Godot:

1. **Navigation2D or NavigationServer:** Use the Navigation2D or NavigationServer class to create navigation meshes or grids that define walkable areas and obstacles in your game world.

2. **NavigationAgent:** Attach NavigationAgent components to entities that need pathfinding capabilities.

3. **NavigationPath:** Request pathfinding by creating a NavigationPath instance and using the compute_path method to find a path from the entity's current position to a target location.

```
# Example of requesting pathfinding in Godot
var path = NavigationPath.new()
if navigation_server.compute_path(path, entity.global_transform.origin, targe
t_position):
    # Path found, follow it
    entity.follow_path(path)
else:
    # No path found, handle accordingly
```

4. **Path Following:** Implement logic to follow the path returned by the pathfinding algorithm. This may involve steering behaviors or waypoint following.

Decision-making is the process by which AI entities choose actions or behaviors in response to the game's state and objectives. Common decision-making techniques include:

1. **Finite State Machines (FSM):** Divide an entity's behavior into discrete states, where each state represents a specific behavior or action. Transitions between states are determined by certain conditions.

2. **Behavior Trees:** Construct hierarchical trees of behaviors where each node represents a specific action, condition, or sequence. Behavior trees offer flexibility and can handle complex decision-making.

3. **Utility-Based AI:** Assign utility values to different actions or behaviors, and have the AI choose the action with the highest utility score. This approach allows for more nuanced decision-making.

4. **Planning and Goal-Oriented AI:** Implement AI that plans a series of actions to achieve a particular goal. Algorithms like A* can be used for this purpose.

```
# Example of a simple finite state machine in Godot
enum AIState { IDLE, PATROL, CHASE, ATTACK }

func _process(delta):
    match current_state:
        AIState.IDLE:
            # Handle idle behavior
        AIState.PATROL:
            # Handle patrol behavior
        AIState.CHASE:
            # Handle chase behavior
        AIState.ATTACK:
            # Handle attack behavior
```

For AI entities to make informed decisions, they need to perceive and react to changes in the game world. Sensory perception can include:

1. **Vision:** Implement line of sight checks to determine if an AI entity can "see" other entities. Use raycasting or visibility checks to simulate vision.

2. **Hearing:** Simulate hearing by detecting sounds or events in the game world. AI entities can react to nearby noises or events.

3. **Awareness and Memory:** AI entities may have a memory system to remember the player's last known position or the locations of important objects.

4. **Proximity and Sensors:** Implement sensors that detect nearby entities or objects. Use triggers or areas of effect to determine proximity.

Balancing AI difficulty is crucial to creating enjoyable gameplay. Consider providing different difficulty levels, adjusting factors such as reaction times, accuracy, and decision-making based on the selected difficulty level. Playtesting and feedback are essential for fine-tuning AI difficulty.

In conclusion, implementing AI in Godot games involves pathfinding algorithms, decision-making techniques, sensory perception, and balancing. AI enhances gameplay by creating dynamic, intelligent, and challenging entities that interact with the game world and the player. Properly designed AI contributes to a more engaging and immersive gaming experience.

10.2 Creating Non-Player Characters (NPCs)

Non-Player Characters (NPCs) are essential elements of many games, providing interaction, storytelling, and challenges. In this section, we'll explore how to create NPCs in Godot, including their behavior, dialogue, and role within the game world.

The Role of NPCs

NPCs serve various roles in games:

1. **Storytelling:** NPCs can deliver plot points, lore, and exposition to players, helping to advance the game's narrative.

2. **Quest Givers:** NPCs can offer quests, missions, or objectives that drive gameplay and provide goals for the player to achieve.

3. **Vendors and Traders:** NPCs can act as shops, allowing players to buy and sell items or equipment.

4. **Enemies and Allies:** NPCs can function as adversaries, enemies, or allies, influencing combat and gameplay dynamics.

Creating NPCs in Godot

To create NPCs in Godot, follow these steps:

1. **Create NPC Scenes:** Design individual NPC characters as scenes within Godot. These scenes may include character models, animations, and associated logic.

Dialogue System: Implement a dialogue system to manage conversations between the player and NPCs.

10.3 Game State Management and Logic

Effective game state management and logic are crucial for creating organized and immersive gameplay experiences in Godot. In this section, we'll explore techniques and best practices for managing game states, handling transitions, and implementing game logic.

The Importance of Game State Management

Game state management involves tracking the current state of the game, such as menus, gameplay, cutscenes, and pause screens. Proper management ensures that the game responds correctly to player input and events, maintains consistency, and delivers a seamless player experience.

Finite State Machines (FSMs)

Finite State Machines (FSMs) are a popular approach to managing game states and logic. In an FSM:

1. **States:** Define discrete states that represent different phases or screens of the game, such as "MainMenu," "Playing," "Paused," "Cutscene," and more.

2. **Transitions:** Specify conditions that trigger transitions between states. Transitions can be based on player input, events, or predefined criteria.

3. **State-specific Logic:** Implement state-specific logic and behaviors within each state. For example, the "MainMenu" state handles menu navigation and options, while the "Playing" state manages gameplay mechanics.

Here's a simplified FSM example in Godot using GDScript:

```
enum GameState { MainMenu, Playing, Paused, GameOver }

# Initialize the game state
var current_state : GameState = GameState.MainMenu

func _process(delta):
    match current_state:
        GameState.MainMenu:
            # Handle main menu logic
        GameState.Playing:
            # Handle gameplay logic
        GameState.Paused:
            # Handle pause screen logic
        GameState.GameOver:
            # Handle game over logic

# Transition to a new state based on an event
func transition_to_state(new_state : GameState):
```

```
    current_state = new_state
    # Perform any necessary setup for the new state
```

Implementing game logic involves defining the rules, behaviors, and mechanics that govern gameplay. Here are key considerations:

1. **Modular Design:** Break down game logic into manageable modules or scripts that handle specific aspects, such as player controls, enemy AI, physics, and scoring.

2. **Input Handling:** Efficiently handle player input, including keyboard, mouse, gamepad, or touchscreen inputs. Godot provides input handling features and event-based input processing.

```
# Example of input handling in Godot
func _input(event):
    if event.is_action_pressed("move_left"):
        # Handle left movement
    elif event.is_action_pressed("move_right"):
        # Handle right movement
    elif event.is_action_pressed("jump"):
        # Handle jumping
```

3. **Event System:** Utilize event systems to facilitate communication between game objects, enabling them to react to events and trigger actions.

4. **Game Rules:** Define clear game rules and mechanics that dictate how the game world behaves, including physics, collision detection, and win/lose conditions.

Godot's scene system simplifies scene and node management, making it easier to organize game logic and transitions. Scenes can represent different levels, screens, or elements of your game.

1. **Level Design:** Create scenes for individual game levels, allowing you to design, test, and iterate on level layouts and gameplay separately.

2. **Menus and UI:** Design menus, HUDs, and user interfaces as separate scenes that can be loaded and unloaded as needed.

3. **Transition Effects:** Implement transition effects between scenes to enhance the player experience when moving between different game states or levels.

```
# Example of transitioning between scenes in Godot
func change_scene(scene_name):
    get_tree().change_scene(scene_name)
```

Saving and Loading Game State

For games that support saving and loading progress, implement a system that manages player data, including saved game states, preferences, and achievements. Godot provides tools for serializing and deserializing data, making it possible to save and load game states efficiently.

```
# Example of saving and loading game state in Godot
func save_game_state():
    var save_data = {}  # Create a dictionary to store game data
    # Populate the dictionary with game data
    save_data["score"] = player_score
    save_data["level"] = current_level
    File.new().store_var(save_data, "saved_game.dat")

func load_game_state():
    var save_data = {}
    var file = File.new()
    if file.file_exists("saved_game.dat"):
        file.open("saved_game.dat", File.READ)
        save_data = file.get_var()
        file.close()
        # Load game data from the dictionary
        player_score = save_data["score"]
        current_level = save_data["level"]
```

Debugging and Testing

Effective debugging and testing are essential during game development. Use Godot's debugging tools, print statements, and profiling to identify and fix issues in your game logic. Test the game thoroughly to ensure that transitions between states, gameplay mechanics, and rules function correctly.

In conclusion, game state management and logic are fundamental aspects of game development in Godot. By implementing finite state machines, modular logic, scene management, saving/loading functionality, and robust testing, you can create organized, engaging, and bug-free gameplay experiences that captivate players.

10.4 Dynamic Gameplay: Randomness and Procedural Generation

Dynamic gameplay adds variety and replayability to games by introducing elements of randomness and procedural generation. In this section, we'll explore how to implement randomness and procedural generation in Godot to create ever-changing and engaging game experiences.

The Role of Randomness

Randomness plays a vital role in games by introducing unpredictability and surprise. It can affect various aspects of gameplay, such as:

1. **Level Design:** Randomly generated levels or environments provide unique challenges and exploration opportunities.

2. **Enemy Behavior:** Randomized enemy actions, spawn locations, and abilities keep encounters fresh and challenging.

3. **Item Drops:** Random item drops and loot tables add excitement to exploration and reward players for their efforts.

4. **Puzzles and Events:** Randomized puzzles or events can create unexpected obstacles or opportunities for players to solve or exploit.

Random Number Generation

Godot provides functions for generating random numbers, making it easy to introduce randomness into your game. The randi() function generates a random integer, while randf() generates a random floating-point number between 0 and 1.

10.5 Scripting Complex Game Behaviors

Scripting complex game behaviors is a fundamental aspect of game development in Godot. It involves creating intricate interactions, mechanics, and systems that define the gameplay experience. In this section, we'll delve into advanced scripting techniques for implementing complex game behaviors in Godot.

Object-Oriented Programming (OOP)

Godot encourages the use of Object-Oriented Programming (OOP) principles for organizing and managing complex game behaviors. OOP allows you to create reusable and modular code, making it easier to maintain and extend your game.

1. **Classes:** Define classes for different game objects and entities. For example, you might create classes for players, enemies, items, and environmental elements.

```
# Example of defining a Player class in Godot
extends KinematicBody2D

class_name Player

# Class variables and methods
```

2. **Inheritance:** Use inheritance to create specialized subclasses. For instance, you can have subclasses of enemies with unique behaviors based on a common enemy class.

```
# Example of inheritance in Godot
class SkeletonEnemy : Enemy:
    # Custom behavior for skeleton enemies
```

3. **Composition:** Compose game objects by combining multiple components. This allows for flexible and modular design.

```
# Example of composition in Godot
class Weapon:
    # Weapon properties and methods

class Player:
    var weapon = Weapon.new()
    # Player properties and methods, including weapon handling
```

State Machines

State machines are effective for managing complex behaviors, especially for characters and entities with multiple states and interactions. Godot provides a visual state machine editor that simplifies the implementation of state-based behavior.

Visual State Machine Editor: Godot's state machine editor allows you to define states and transitions visually.

11.2 Creating Cutscenes and Cinematics

In this section, we'll dive into the creation of cutscenes and cinematics in Godot, which are essential for storytelling and enhancing the narrative elements of your game. Cutscenes allow you to take control of the camera and game objects to present a scripted sequence, while cinematics typically involve scripted animations, camera movements, and dialogue to advance the plot or provide immersive storytelling.

Cutscenes and cinematics can greatly enhance the player's engagement with your game. They can be used for introductory sequences, dramatic moments, dialogues between characters, and much more. Let's explore how you can create captivating cutscenes and cinematics in Godot.

11.2.1 Creating a Cutscene

Creating a cutscene involves orchestrating the movement and actions of characters and objects in your game world. Here's a step-by-step guide to creating a basic cutscene:

2. **Create a New Scene:** Start by creating a new scene for your cutscene. This scene will contain all the elements and animations required for the cutscene.

Design the Scene: Design the environment and position characters and objects as needed for the cutscene.

11.3 Skeletal and Bone-Based Animation

Skeletal animation, also known as bone-based animation, is a technique widely used in game development to animate characters and objects more efficiently and realistically. Instead of animating the entire mesh or sprite, skeletal animation involves creating a hierarchical structure of bones (also known as joints) within the character or object and animating those bones. This method allows for more natural and dynamic movements, making it a crucial tool for character animation in games. In this section, we'll explore how to implement skeletal animation in Godot.

11.3.1 The Basics of Skeletal Animation

In skeletal animation, you break down your character or object into a hierarchy of bones or joints connected like a skeleton. Each bone has its transformation, and you animate these bones to achieve the desired movement. This approach is especially useful for characters with articulated limbs, as it allows you to control their movements more realistically.

11.3.2 Creating Skeletal Rigs

To start with skeletal animation in Godot, you need to set up a skeletal rig. Here are the general steps:

3. **Create Bones:** In your 2D or 3D modeling software (e.g., Blender), create a skeleton by defining bones and their connections within your character or object.

4. **Rigging:** Assign vertices or parts of your character's mesh to the corresponding bones. This process is known as rigging. Each bone influences the movement of specific parts of the character's mesh.

5. **Export:** Export your character model along with the skeleton and rigging information in a format that Godot can import, such as Collada (DAE) or Godot's own scene format (TSCN).

11.3.3 Importing the Skeletal Rig into Godot

Once you have your character model with the skeletal rig prepared, follow these steps to import it into Godot:

6. **Create a New Scene:** Start by creating a new scene in Godot where you want to place your character.

7. **Import the Model:** Use the "Import" option in the Scene tab to import your character model (usually in DAE or TSCN format).

8. **Attach Skeleton:** Select the imported model and assign the skeleton (skeletal rig) to it. Godot will recognize the bones and their hierarchy.

Skinning and Mesh: Ensure that the character's mesh is properly linked to the bones.

11.4 Facial Animation and Lip Syncing Techniques

Facial animation and lip syncing are crucial for bringing characters to life in games, making their interactions and dialogues more immersive and engaging. In this section, we'll explore techniques and tools for creating facial animations and synchronizing character lip movements with dialogue in Godot.

Facial animation often involves manipulating a character's face to convey emotions, speech, and expressions. In Godot, this is achieved through the use of facial blendshapes or morph targets. These are pre-defined shapes or states of a character's face that can be blended together to create different expressions and lip movements.

To implement facial animation with blendshapes:

9. **Create Blendshapes:** In your modeling software, create a set of blendshapes representing various facial expressions, such as smiling, frowning, and blinking.

10. **Import Blendshapes:** Import your character model along with its blendshapes into Godot. These blendshapes should be part of the character's mesh.

Blendshape Animation: In Godot, you can use the `MeshInstance` node's `set_mesh` method to blend between different blendshape states.

11.5 Integrating Animation with Game Logic

Integrating animation with game logic is a crucial aspect of game development, as it allows you to create interactive and dynamic experiences. In this section, we'll explore how to synchronize and control animations within the broader context of your game using Godot's scripting capabilities.

11.5.1 Animation Player Node

Godot provides the "AnimationPlayer" node, which is a versatile tool for managing animations and their interactions with game logic. Here are the key steps to integrate animation with game logic using the AnimationPlayer:

Creating Animations: First, create animations for your game elements using the AnimationPlayer's editor.

Chapter 12: Mobile Game Development

12.1 Adapting Games for Mobile Platforms

Mobile game development is a thriving sector of the gaming industry, offering immense opportunities for developers to reach a vast and diverse audience. Adapting your games for mobile platforms requires careful consideration of hardware limitations, user interaction, and platform-specific features. In this section, we'll explore the key aspects of adapting games for mobile devices using Godot.

12.1.1 Understanding Mobile Platforms

Mobile platforms, such as iOS and Android, have unique characteristics that influence game development:

- **Screen Size and Resolution:** Mobile devices come in various screen sizes and resolutions. Design your game's user interface (UI) to be responsive and adaptable to different screen dimensions.

- **Touch Controls:** Unlike traditional gaming platforms with physical controllers, mobile devices rely on touch screens for input. Design intuitive touch controls that suit your game's mechanics.

- **Performance Variability:** Mobile devices vary in processing power and capabilities. Optimize your game for performance to ensure smooth gameplay on a range of devices.

- **Battery Life:** Games can be resource-intensive and drain a device's battery quickly. Implement power-efficient coding practices to minimize battery consumption.

- **App Store Guidelines:** Mobile games must adhere to app store guidelines for distribution. Familiarize yourself with these guidelines to ensure your game can be published.

12.1.2 Porting

12.5 Ensuring Game Accessibility and Inclusivity

Ensuring that your mobile game is accessible and inclusive is not only ethically important but also beneficial for reaching a broader audience and enhancing the overall player experience. In this section, we'll explore the key aspects of making your Godot mobile game accessible to a wide range of players, including those with disabilities.

12.5.1 Accessibility Features

Implementing accessibility features in your mobile game is a significant step toward inclusivity. Here are some essential accessibility features to consider:

11. **Text-to-Speech (TTS):** Provide an option for text-based content, such as menus and dialogues, to be read aloud using TTS functionality. Make sure to include descriptions for UI elements.

12. **High Contrast Mode:** Offer a high contrast mode with distinct color schemes to improve visibility for players with visual impairments.

13. **Customizable Fonts and Text Sizes:** Allow players to adjust font styles, sizes, and colors to suit their visual preferences and needs.

14. **Subtitles and Closed Captions:** Include subtitles for in-game dialogue and provide closed captions for important audio cues and narrative elements.

15. **Button Remapping:** Allow players to customize control inputs, including button remapping, to accommodate their preferred control scheme or physical limitations.

16. **Colorblind Modes:** Implement colorblind-friendly design options to ensure that players with color vision deficiencies can discern critical game elements.

17. **Easy Mode:** Offer an easy mode or adjustable difficulty settings for players who may require less challenging gameplay.

18. **Sensitivity and Speed Settings:** Provide options to adjust sensitivity and input speed for touch controls, gyroscopic controls, or other input methods.

12.5.2

Chapter 13: Virtual Reality and Augmented Reality

13.1 Introduction to VR and AR in Godot

Virtual Reality (VR) and Augmented Reality (AR) are cutting-edge technologies that have the potential to revolutionize the way we experience games and applications. In this section, we'll introduce you to VR and AR development in Godot and provide an overview of the key concepts and tools.

What is Virtual Reality (VR)?

Virtual Reality (VR) is a technology that immerses users in a computer-generated, three-dimensional environment. VR typically involves the use of a headset, which tracks the user's head movements and displays stereoscopic 3D visuals to create the illusion of being inside a virtual world. VR experiences can range from immersive games and simulations to educational and training applications.

What is Augmented Reality (AR)?

Augmented Reality (AR) blends digital content with the real world, enhancing the user's perception of reality. Unlike VR, AR does not require a headset that completely blocks out the real world. Instead, AR applications often use smartphones or AR glasses to overlay digital elements onto the user's view of the physical environment. AR has applications in gaming, navigation, education, and more.

VR and AR in Godot

Godot Engine has made significant strides in supporting VR and AR development. Here's what you need to know about VR and AR in Godot:

VR Support

Godot provides VR support through the OpenVR GDNative plugin, which allows you to create VR experiences compatible with a wide range of VR headsets, including the HTC Vive, Oculus Rift, and Valve Index.

To get started with VR development in Godot, you'll need to install the OpenVR GDNative plugin and configure your project to use VR settings. Godot provides built-in nodes and functions for handling VR input, tracking controllers, and rendering for VR headsets.

AR Support

As of my knowledge cutoff date in January 2022, Godot's built-in support for AR is limited, and you may need to rely on third-party plugins or extensions to implement AR features. However, the field of AR development is rapidly evolving, and it's possible that Godot's AR capabilities have advanced further since that time. Be sure to check the official Godot documentation and community resources for the latest information on AR support in Godot.

Developing VR and AR applications often involves specialized tools and hardware. Here are some essential tools and components you may need:

- **VR Headsets:** Depending on your target platform, you'll need VR headsets compatible with your development environment.

- **AR Devices:** For AR development, consider devices like AR-capable smartphones, tablets, or AR glasses.

- **Development Environment:** Set up the appropriate development environment for VR and AR. For Godot, you'll need to configure the engine to work with VR headsets and potentially AR plugins.

- **3D Modeling Software:** VR and AR applications often require 3D models and assets. Tools like Blender, Maya, or Godot's built-in 3D editor can help with modeling and asset creation.

- **AR SDKs and Plugins:** If you're working with AR, you may need to integrate AR software development kits (SDKs) or plugins for your target platforms.

- **VR Controllers:** If your VR experience involves hand interaction, you'll need to develop or obtain VR controllers compatible with your VR headset.

In the following subsections, we'll delve deeper into VR and AR development in Godot, including setting up a VR project, working with VR input, and considerations for AR development.

Stay updated with the latest developments in VR and AR technology, as the field continues to advance, and new opportunities for game development and interactive experiences emerge.

13.2 Setting Up VR and AR Environments

Setting up virtual reality (VR) and augmented reality (AR) environments in Godot requires specific configurations and considerations. In this section, we'll explore how to prepare your development environment and Godot project for VR and AR development.

VR Environment Setup

Before you can start developing VR experiences in Godot, you need to set up your VR environment. Here are the steps to get you started:

19. **VR Hardware:** Ensure that you have compatible VR hardware, such as a VR headset (e.g., Oculus Rift, HTC Vive, Valve Index) and motion controllers if needed.

20. **Install Godot VR Plugin:** Godot provides VR support through the OpenVR GDNative plugin. Install this plugin by following the official instructions provided in the Godot documentation. The plugin allows Godot to communicate with your VR hardware.

21. **Configure Project Settings:** Open your Godot project and navigate to "Project" -> "Project Settings." Under the "Common" section, select the "Application" tab. Here, you can enable VR support by checking the "Virtual Reality" checkbox.

22. **Import VR-Specific Assets:** If your VR project requires 3D models, textures, or assets specific to VR, make sure to import and configure them accordingly. Pay attention to the scale and dimensions of your assets to ensure they appear correctly in the VR environment.

23. **Enable VR Camera:** Create or configure a camera in your 3D scene that's set up to work with VR. In the camera settings, set the "Current" property to "Enabled."

24. **Implement VR Interactions:** Depending on your VR project, you'll need to implement interactions with the VR controllers. Godot provides functions and nodes for tracking VR controllers and handling input events.

25. **Test in VR:** Connect your VR headset, launch your Godot project, and test your VR experience. Ensure that the VR environment is rendering correctly and that interactions work as intended.

AR Environment Setup

As of my last knowledge update in January 2022, Godot's built-in support for AR is limited, and you may need to rely on third-party plugins or extensions to implement AR features. Here are the general steps for setting up an AR environment in Godot:

26. **Select AR Platform:** Choose the AR platform you want to target, such as ARCore for Android or ARKit for iOS. Make sure to familiarize yourself with the platform's development requirements and SDKs.

27. **Install AR Plugin:** If available, install an AR plugin or extension for Godot that supports the AR platform you've selected. These plugins typically provide the necessary tools and nodes for AR development.

28. **Configure Project Settings:** Access your Godot project's settings and configure them to support AR. This may involve specifying AR-related settings, such as camera configurations and tracking modes.

29. **Create AR Scene:** Set up your AR scene within Godot. This scene should include elements and nodes specific to AR, such as AR anchors, camera tracking, and 3D models or objects that interact with the real world.

30. **Implement AR Interactions:** Write scripts and logic to handle AR interactions. This may include detecting real-world objects or surfaces, placing virtual objects in the AR environment, and responding to user interactions.

31. **Test on AR Device:** Connect a compatible AR device (e.g., AR-capable smartphone or tablet) to your development environment. Deploy your Godot AR project to the device and test its functionality in a real-world environment.

32. **Iterate and Optimize:** Iterate on your AR project, fine-tuning interactions and optimizing performance. Ensure that your AR experience is responsive and visually appealing in different real-world scenarios.

Please note that the field of AR development is rapidly evolving, and the availability of AR tools and plugins for Godot may have expanded since my last knowledge update. Be sure to consult the official Godot documentation and relevant community resources for the most up-to-date information on AR development in Godot.

Setting up VR and AR environments in Godot can be an exciting but technically challenging endeavor. Be prepared to invest time in learning the specific requirements of your chosen VR or AR platform and experimenting with interactions to create engaging and immersive experiences for users.

13.3 Designing Immersive VR/AR Experiences

Designing immersive virtual reality (VR) and augmented reality (AR) experiences in Godot requires a deep understanding of the unique opportunities and challenges these technologies present. In this section, we'll explore the principles and best practices for creating compelling VR and AR content.

Principles of Immersive VR/AR Design

33. **Presence:** The primary goal of VR is to create a sense of presence, where users feel like they are physically present in the virtual environment. To achieve this, pay attention to realistic scale, depth perception, and interactivity.

13.4 Performance and Optimization for VR/AR

Performance optimization is crucial when developing virtual reality (VR) and augmented reality (AR) experiences in Godot. To provide smooth and immersive experiences, you must ensure that your project runs efficiently on the target hardware. In this section, we'll delve into performance considerations and optimization techniques for VR and AR development.

Hardware Limitations

VR and AR experiences place significant demands on hardware, and different devices have varying capabilities. Here are some hardware-related factors to consider:

- **Processing Power:** VR/AR headsets and mobile devices have limited processing power compared to desktop computers. Optimize your code to run efficiently on these platforms.

- **Graphics Rendering:** Maintain a consistent frame rate (e.g., 90 FPS) to prevent motion sickness in VR. Implement performance-efficient rendering techniques like occlusion culling and level of detail (LOD).

- **Memory Constraints:** Mobile devices often have limited RAM. Optimize memory usage by reducing the size of textures, minimizing unnecessary asset loading, and implementing efficient resource management.

Performance Optimization Techniques

34. **GPU Optimization:** Utilize techniques like frustum culling to avoid rendering objects outside the user's view. Implement occlusion culling to skip rendering objects hidden by others. Godot provides tools for these optimizations.

35. **LOD (Level of Detail):** Create multiple versions of 3D models with varying levels of detail. Use the appropriate LOD based on the object's distance from the user to reduce polygon count and texture resolution.

36. **Texture Compression:** Compress textures to reduce memory usage and improve loading times. Use formats like ETC2 for Android and PVRTC for iOS.

37. **Asset Streaming:** Implement asset streaming to load assets on-demand instead of preloading everything at the start. This minimizes initial loading times and memory usage.

38. **Baking Lighting:** Bake static lighting and shadows whenever possible, reducing the real-time rendering workload. Use Godot's light baking system for efficient lighting.

39. **Script Optimization:** Profile your scripts to identify bottlenecks. Optimize critical code sections, use efficient algorithms, and minimize unnecessary calculations.

40. **Multithreading:** Utilize Godot's multithreading capabilities to offload heavy tasks to separate threads, improving overall performance.

41. **Particle Systems:** Be mindful of the complexity of particle systems. Use particle pooling to efficiently reuse particles and reduce CPU load.

42. **Streaming and LOD for Large Environments:** In expansive VR/AR environments, implement terrain streaming and LOD for distant objects to maintain performance.

13.5 Integrating Real-World Elements into AR Games

Augmented Reality (AR) games provide unique opportunities to blend virtual experiences with the real world. In this section, we'll explore techniques and considerations for integrating real-world elements into your AR games developed with Godot.

Recognizing Real-World Objects

One of the key features of AR is the ability to recognize and interact with real-world objects. To achieve this, consider the following:

43. **Image Recognition:** Implement image recognition to detect specific images or patterns in the real world. When the AR camera identifies these markers, you can trigger virtual interactions or animations.

    ```
    # Example: Using the ARMarkerDetector node in Godot to detect an image
    marker.
    extends ARMarkerDetector

    func _on_MarkerDetected(marker_id):
        # Handle marker detection, e.g., spawn virtual objects or trigger a
    ctions.
    ```

44. **Object Tracking:** Track the position and movement of real-world objects using ARKit or ARCore APIs. This allows you to place virtual objects on and interact with physical objects.

    ```
    # Example: Tracking an object's movement in Godot AR.
    extends ARVRAnchor

    func _process(delta):
        # Update the virtual object's position based on the tracked anchor.
    ```

Real-World Interaction

Enhance user engagement by enabling interactions between virtual and real-world elements:

45. **Object Interaction:** Enable users to interact with physical objects by tapping, dragging, or attaching virtual objects to them. For instance, users can place virtual decorations on their physical furniture.

46. **Physical Feedback:** Implement haptic feedback or visual cues when users interact with real-world objects. This provides a sense of responsiveness and immersion.

    ```
    # Example: Triggering haptic feedback in Godot AR.
    func _on_InteractButtonPressed():
        if ARVRController.has_haptic_feedback():
            ARVRController.trigger_haptic_feedback(0.5, 0.5)
    ```

47. **Object Physics:** Apply physics to virtual objects so they can collide with and react to real-world objects. Use Godot's physics engine to create realistic interactions.

```
# Example: Applying physics to a virtual object in Godot AR.
func _physics_process(delta):
    var collision_info = move_and_collide(velocity * delta)
    if collision_info:
        # Handle collision with the real world.
    ```
```

## Geolocation-Based AR

Incorporate geolocation data into your AR games to provide location-based experiences:

48. **GPS Data:** Access GPS data to determine the user's real-world location. Use this information to trigger events or spawn virtual content specific to their location.

49. **Map Integration:** Overlay a map of the user's surroundings with AR annotations, such as points of interest or navigation cues.

50. **Geo-Fencing:** Define virtual boundaries or "geo-fences" that trigger actions when users enter specific geographic areas.

## Real-World Data Visualization

AR allows you to visualize real-world data in innovative ways:

51. **Data Overlays:** Display real-time data overlays on top of the user's view. For example, in an astronomy AR app, you could show constellations as users point their devices at the night sky.

52. **Information Retrieval:** Use object recognition to retrieve information about real-world objects. Pointing a device at a book could provide details about the book, its author, and related information.

## Privacy and Permissions

When integrating real-world elements into AR games, respect user privacy and obtain necessary permissions for accessing device features such as the camera, GPS, and microphone. Clearly communicate how data will be used and stored to build trust with your users.

## Cross-Platform Considerations

Consider the platform-specific AR frameworks (e.g., ARKit for iOS, ARCore for Android) when developing AR games. Each platform may have its own features and capabilities, so tailor your game accordingly for a consistent user experience.

Integrating real-world elements into AR games opens up exciting possibilities for immersive and location-aware experiences. Whether you're recognizing real-world objects,
```

enabling interactions, or visualizing data, Godot provides a versatile platform for creating engaging AR games that merge the virtual and physical worlds.

Chapter 14: Testing and Quality Assurance

14.1 Developing a Testing Strategy

Testing is a critical phase in the game development process that ensures your game functions as intended, is free of critical bugs, and provides an enjoyable experience for players. In this section, we'll explore the importance of testing and how to develop a comprehensive testing strategy for your Godot game.

The Importance of Testing

Testing serves several crucial purposes in game development:

53. **Bug Detection:** Testing helps identify and fix bugs, glitches, and errors in your game. Addressing these issues early prevents them from reaching players and negatively impacting their experience.

54. **Quality Assurance:** Testing ensures that your game meets quality standards and is free of game-breaking issues. It helps maintain a positive reputation and player satisfaction.

55. **Balancing and Tuning:** Through testing, you can fine-tune gameplay mechanics, difficulty levels, and balance to provide a rewarding and enjoyable experience.

56. **Compatibility:** Testing across various platforms and devices ensures your game works correctly on different hardware and operating systems.

14.2 Automated Testing and Continuous Integration

Automated testing and continuous integration (CI) are essential practices in game development that help ensure the stability, quality, and reliability of your Godot game. In this section, we'll explore the concepts of automated testing and CI and how to implement them effectively.

Automated Testing

Automated testing involves using scripts and tools to execute tests automatically, verifying that different aspects of your game function correctly. Godot supports automated testing through its built-in testing framework, which allows you to write and run test cases using GDScript.

Writing Automated Tests

Here's an example of a simple automated test case in GDScript:

```
# Example: Writing an automated test in GDScript.
func test_addition():
    assert(2 + 2 == 4, "2 + 2 should equal 4")
```

In this example, the `assert` statement checks if the addition operation results in the expected value. If the condition is false, an error message is displayed.

Running Automated Tests

14.3 Beta Testing and

14.4 Debugging and Troubleshooting Common Issues

Debugging is an essential skill in game development that involves identifying and fixing issues or errors in your Godot game's code, behavior, or functionality. In this section, we'll explore common debugging techniques and strategies to troubleshoot issues effectively.

The Debugging Process

Debugging typically follows a systematic process to pinpoint and resolve problems:

57. **Reproduction:** First, reproduce the issue consistently. Ensure that you can trigger the problem reliably, as this makes debugging much easier.

58. **Observation:** Use debugging tools and techniques to observe the game's behavior. This may include checking variables, logging data, or using visual debugging tools.

59. **Hypothesis:** Formulate a hypothesis about the cause of the issue based on your observations. Consider what part of the code might be responsible.

60. **Testing:** Test your hypothesis by making changes to the code. This might involve adding print statements, modifying variables, or using debugging features.

61. **Verification:** Verify whether your changes have resolved the issue. If not, revise your hypothesis and repeat the process until the problem is resolved.

Common Debugging Techniques

1. Logging and Print Statements:
```
# Example: Using print statements for debugging.
func _process(delta):
    print("Player position:", player.global_position)
```

Logging helps track variable values, function execution flow, and error messages. The output can be viewed in the Godot editor's output panel.

2. Breakpoints:

Set breakpoints in your code, which pause execution when reached.

14.5 Ensuring Game Accessibility and Inclusivity

Game accessibility and inclusivity are essential considerations in modern game development. Ensuring that your Godot game is accessible to a wide range of players, including those with disabilities, enhances the overall gaming experience and broadens your potential audience. In this section, we'll explore the importance of accessibility and inclusivity and provide guidelines for implementing them in your game.

Why Accessibility Matters

Accessibility is about making your game usable and enjoyable by all players, regardless of their abilities or disabilities. Here are some reasons why accessibility is crucial:

62. **Inclusivity:** Games that are accessible welcome a broader and more diverse player base, fostering inclusivity and promoting a positive gaming community.

63. **Legal Compliance:** In some regions, there are legal requirements for software, including games, to be accessible to people with disabilities. Complying with these regulations is essential.

64. **Social Responsibility:** Game developers have a responsibility to ensure that their creations are accessible to as many people as possible.

Guidelines for Game Accessibility

1.

15.1 Profiling and Identifying Performance Bottlenecks

Performance optimization is a critical aspect of game development to ensure your Godot game runs smoothly and provides an enjoyable player experience. Profiling is the process of analyzing your game's performance to identify bottlenecks and areas for improvement. In this section, we'll explore profiling techniques and tools in Godot to help you identify and address performance issues.

Why Profiling Matters

Profiling is essential for the following reasons:

1. **Optimizing Gameplay:** Profiling helps you discover performance bottlenecks that can cause lag, stuttering, or low frame rates during gameplay.

2. **Consistency:** By optimizing your game's performance, you ensure that it runs smoothly across different hardware configurations and devices.

3. **Resource Efficiency:** Profiling helps reduce resource consumption, leading to longer battery life on mobile devices and less strain on players' hardware.

Profiling Techniques

1. FPS Monitoring:

FPS (Frames Per Second) monitoring is the most basic form of profiling. In Godot, you can enable the FPS monitor in the editor to see the current frame rate and identify any significant drops in performance.

```
# Enable FPS monitoring in Godot.
ProjectSettings.monitoring/quality/debug/fps_monitor = true
```

2. Frame Profiling:

Frame profiling allows you to measure the time taken by different parts of a single frame's processing. Godot provides built-in frame profiling tools that display how much time each node, script, or function consumes during a frame.

```
# Enable frame profiling in Godot.
ProjectSettings.monitoring/quality/debug/profile_frames = true
```

3. Profiler Tab:

The Profiler tab in the Godot editor provides a detailed breakdown of resource usage, including memory, CPU, and rendering performance. It helps you identify which parts of your game are consuming the most resources.

4. Remote Profiling:

Godot supports remote profiling, allowing you to profile a game running on a different device or platform. This is particularly useful for testing performance on target platforms.

Identifying Bottlenecks

Once you've enabled profiling and collected performance data, you can start identifying bottlenecks and performance issues:

1. **High Frame Time:** Look for nodes or functions that have high frame time percentages. These are potential bottlenecks that need optimization.

2. **Resource Consumption:** Check the memory and CPU usage of different parts of your game. Identify areas where resources are being used inefficiently.

3. **Rendering Overhead:** Assess rendering performance, including the number of draw calls and shader complexity. Reducing unnecessary rendering can significantly improve performance.

4. **Scripting Optimization:** Optimize your scripts by reducing unnecessary calculations, minimizing object creation, and avoiding expensive operations within loops.

Once you've identified performance bottlenecks, consider the following optimization strategies:

1. **Data-Driven Design:** Use data-driven design principles to minimize hardcoding and enable easier optimization.

2. **Resource Management:** Implement resource management techniques to load and unload assets efficiently.

3. **Streaming and LOD:** Use techniques like level-of-detail (LOD) and streaming to manage resource loading dynamically.

4. **Multithreading:** Take advantage of Godot's multithreading capabilities to offload resource-intensive tasks to separate threads.

5. **Asset Compression:** Compress textures and audio files to reduce their size and memory usage.

6. **Shader Optimization:** Optimize shaders by reducing complexity and avoiding unnecessary calculations.

7. **Profile Iteratively:** Profile and optimize your game iteratively, focusing on the most critical bottlenecks first.

Conclusion

Profiling and performance optimization are essential aspects of Godot game development. By enabling profiling tools, identifying bottlenecks, and implementing optimization strategies, you can ensure that your game delivers a smooth and enjoyable experience to players on various platforms and devices. Regularly monitor and profile your game, especially when adding new features or making significant changes, to maintain optimal performance throughout the development process.

15.2 Techniques for Optimizing Game Speed

Optimizing game speed is crucial for delivering a smooth and responsive gaming experience to players. In this section, we'll explore various techniques and best practices for optimizing the speed and performance of your Godot game.

Why Game Speed Matters

Game speed, often measured in frames per second (FPS), directly impacts the playability and enjoyability of your game. A high and consistent FPS ensures that gameplay is fluid and responsive, while a low FPS can result in laggy and frustrating gameplay. Here are some reasons why game speed matters:

1. **Player Experience:** A smooth and fast game feels more engaging and enjoyable, immersing players in the game world.

2. **Responsiveness:** Responsive controls and quick feedback are essential for a satisfying gaming experience.

3. **Competitive Advantage:** In competitive multiplayer games, a higher FPS can provide a competitive advantage by reducing input lag.

Optimization Techniques

1. Draw Call Reduction:
- Minimize the number of draw calls by using techniques like batching and instancing.
- Use the "Visible" property on nodes to control when they are drawn.

2. Texture Compression:
- Compress textures to reduce memory usage and load times.
- Use texture atlases to combine multiple textures into one, reducing draw calls.

3. Level of Detail (LOD):
- Implement LOD systems for models and objects to reduce the level of detail when objects are distant from the camera.

4. Culling:
- Use frustum culling to avoid rendering objects that are not within the camera's view.
- Implement occlusion culling to skip rendering of objects that are hidden by other objects.

5. Script Optimization:
- Optimize scripts by avoiding unnecessary calculations and expensive operations.
- Use profiling tools to identify performance bottlenecks in your scripts.

6. Multithreading:
- Offload resource-intensive tasks to separate threads using Godot's multithreading capabilities.

7. Asset Streaming:
- Implement asset streaming to load and unload resources dynamically as needed.
- Use asynchronous loading for large assets to prevent frame rate drops.

8. Physics Optimization:
- Optimize physics calculations by adjusting physics properties and using simpler collision shapes when appropriate.

9. Shader Optimization:

- Optimize shaders by reducing complexity and avoiding costly calculations.
- Use shader quality settings to provide different levels of visual fidelity.

10. Resource Pooling:

- Implement resource pooling to reuse objects, such as bullets or enemies, in stead of constantly creating and destroying them.

11. Delta Time:

- Use delta time (elapsed time since the last frame) for time-based calculati ons to ensure consistent behavior across different frame rates.

12. Asset Size Reduction:

- Compress audio files and reduce their quality to save memory.
- Use procedural generation or tile-based maps to reduce the size of levels.

13. Platform-Specific Optimization:

- Optimize your game for specific target platforms, considering their hardwar e capabilities and limitations.

14. Regular Profiling:

- Profile your game regularly to identify performance bottlenecks and address them proactively.

Benchmarking and Testing

Benchmarking involves running your game on various devices and hardware configurations to assess its performance. Testing on different platforms helps ensure that your game runs smoothly on a wide range of systems.

Consider conducting user testing and collecting feedback from players to identify performance issues and areas for improvement. Player feedback can be invaluable in fine-tuning your game's performance.

Conclusion

Optimizing game speed is an ongoing process that involves a combination of techniques, tools, and testing. By following these optimization techniques and best practices, you can create a fast and responsive Godot game that provides an excellent gaming experience to players across different platforms and devices. Regular profiling and testing are key to maintaining optimal performance throughout the development and release of your game.

15.3 Balancing Graphics Quality and Performance

Balancing graphics quality and performance is a critical aspect of game development, especially when targeting a wide range of hardware configurations. In this section, we'll explore strategies and techniques for achieving the right balance between visual fidelity and smooth performance in your Godot game.

The Importance of Graphics Quality and Performance

Graphics quality and performance play a significant role in shaping the player's experience. While high-quality visuals enhance immersion and engagement, smooth performance ensures responsive gameplay. Achieving the right balance is essential to cater to different player preferences and hardware capabilities.

Techniques for Balancing Graphics Quality

1. *Graphics Settings:*
   - Implement a range of graphics settings in your game, including options for resolution, texture quality, shadows, and post-processing effects.
   - Allow players to customize these settings to match their hardware capabilities and preferences.

2. *Dynamic Resolution Scaling:*
   - Implement dynamic resolution scaling to adjust the rendering resolution based on the player's hardware. This can help maintain a consistent frame rate.

3. *Level of Detail (LOD):*
   - Use LOD techniques to reduce the level of detail in distant objects, optimizing performance without sacrificing close-up visual quality.

4. *Texture Streaming:*
   - Implement texture streaming to load high-resolution textures only when they are needed, reducing memory usage and load times.

5. *Shader Quality Levels:*
   - Provide different shader quality levels that players can choose from. Lower-quality shaders can significantly improve performance.

6. *Anti-Aliasing Options:*
   - Offer various anti-aliasing options, such as FXAA or MSAA, for players to choose from based on their hardware capabilities.

7. *Frame Rate Caps:*
   - Allow players to cap the maximum frame rate, which can help reduce GPU usage on high-refresh-rate monitors.

Performance Monitoring

To effectively balance graphics quality and performance, it's crucial to monitor performance metrics during development and testing. Use Godot's profiling tools, FPS monitoring, and frame analysis to identify areas of improvement.

1. Frame Timing Analysis:

- Analyze the time spent on different rendering phases, such as CPU time, GPU time, and idle time, to pinpoint performance bottlenecks.

2. Memory Usage:

- Keep an eye on memory usage to ensure that your game doesn't exceed hardware limitations.

3. GPU Profiling:

- Use GPU profiling tools to identify which shaders and rendering processes consume the most GPU resources.

4. Benchmarking:

- Benchmark your game on various hardware configurations to assess performance and graphics quality across a spectrum of devices.

Platform-Specific Considerations

Graphics quality and performance considerations can vary depending on the target platform. Be mindful of the hardware limitations and capabilities of the platforms you're developing for. Mobile devices, for example, may require more aggressive optimization than high-end gaming PCs.

15.4 Memory Management and Resource Handling

Efficient memory management and resource handling are critical for the overall performance and stability of your Godot game. In this section, we'll explore techniques and best practices for managing memory and handling resources effectively.

Why Memory Management Matters

Memory management is essential for the following reasons:

1. **Stability:** Proper memory management prevents memory leaks and crashes, ensuring that your game runs smoothly without unexpected interruptions.

2. **Performance:** Efficient memory usage improves game performance by reducing overhead and preventing unnecessary resource loading.

3. **Resource Conservation:** Effective memory management conserves system resources, extending the playability of your game on a wider range of devices.

Techniques for Memory Management

1. Resource Unloading:

- Unload resources that are no longer needed to free up memory. Godot provides methods like `ResourceLoader.unload` to release resources explicitly.

```
# Unload a resource when it's no longer needed.
var myTexture = preload("res://textures/my_texture.png")
ResourceLoader.unload(myTexture)
```

2. *Object Pooling:*

- Implement object pooling for frequently created and destroyed objects, such as bullets or enemies. Reusing objects reduces memory allocation and deallocation overhead.

```
# Example of object pooling in Godot.
func _on_SpawnTimer_timeout():
    var bullet = get_bullet_from_pool()
    bullet.position = spawn_point
    bullet.shoot()
```

3. *Streaming and Asynchronous Loading:*

- Use streaming and asynchronous loading to load resources on-demand. This prevents long loading times and reduces memory consumption.

```
# Asynchronously load a scene.
var scene = load("res://scenes/my_scene.tscn", true)
```

4. *Resource Preloading:*

- Preload essential resources at the start of the game or when transitioning between scenes. Preloaded resources remain in memory until explicitly unloaded.

```
# Preload resources at the start of the game.
var myTexture = preload("res://textures/my_texture.png")
```

5. *Resource Dependencies:*

- Be aware of resource dependencies. If a resource depends on another, unloading the parent resource should also unload its dependencies to avoid memory leaks.

6. *Manual Memory Management:*

- For advanced scenarios, you can manage memory manually using GDScript's push_error_handler and pop_error_handler to catch and handle memory allocation errors.

```
# Example of manual memory management.
push_error_handler()
var customResource = ResourceClass.new()
pop_error_handler()
```

Resource Handling Best Practices

1. *Resource Organization:*

- Organize your project's resources into folders and use a consistent naming convention to make it easier to manage and locate assets.

2. Resource Compression:

- Compress audio and texture resources to reduce their size, saving memory and storage space.

3. Texture Atlases:

- Combine multiple textures into atlases to reduce draw calls and memory overhead.

4. Streaming Zones:

- Implement streaming zones in large open-world games to load and unload portions of the game world as the player moves, optimizing memory usage.

5. Clean-Up on Scene Change:

- Explicitly clean up resources when changing scenes to ensure that resources from the previous scene are released.

Conclusion

Effective memory management and resource handling are fundamental for maintaining a stable and high-performing Godot game. By following these techniques and best practices, you can optimize memory usage, prevent memory leaks, and ensure a smooth gaming experience for your players. Regularly review and profile your game to identify and address any memory-related issues as your project evolves.

15.5 Cross-Platform Performance Considerations

Developing a cross-platform game with Godot involves optimizing your game to run smoothly on a variety of devices, operating systems, and hardware configurations. In this section, we'll explore considerations and strategies for achieving excellent cross-platform performance.

The Challenge of Cross-Platform Development

Cross-platform game development presents unique challenges due to the diversity of devices and performance capabilities. What works well on a high-end gaming PC may struggle on a mobile device or a low-end computer. Consider the following factors when optimizing for cross-platform performance:

1. Hardware Variability:

Different devices have varying CPU, GPU, memory, and storage capabilities.

16.2 Advanced Lighting and Shadow Techniques

In this section, we'll delve deeper into advanced lighting and shadow techniques available in Godot. Lighting and shadows play a crucial role in creating immersive and visually appealing game environments.

Dynamic Lighting

Dynamic lighting is essential for creating realistic and interactive scenes. Godot supports various types of dynamic lights, including point lights, directional lights, and spotlights. These lights can be moved, rotated, and adjusted in real-time to illuminate your game world dynamically.

Here's a simple example of creating a dynamic point light in GDScript:

```
# Create a new PointLight2D node
var light = PointLight2D.new()

# Set light properties
light.energy = 10.0  # Intensity of the light
light.color = Color(1.0, 1.0, 1.0)  # Light color (white)

# Position the light in the scene
light.position = Vector2(100, 100)

# Add the light to the scene
add_child(light)
```

Shadows

Shadows add depth and realism to your scenes. Godot's 2D and 3D engines support shadow casting and receiving.

16.3 Creating Realistic Materials and Textures

In this section, we will explore the art of creating realistic materials and textures for your game objects in Godot. Realistic materials are essential for immersing players in your game world, making objects look believable and appealing.

Material Properties

Materials in Godot define how the surface of an object interacts with light. To create realistic materials, you need to consider several properties:

- **Albedo (Diffuse Color):** This property represents the base color of the material. It defines how the material reflects or absorbs different colors of light. Realistic materials have albedo values that match their real-world counterparts.

- **Specular and Glossiness:** These properties control the reflection of light. A specular map defines where light is reflected strongly or weakly, while glossiness determines how sharp or blurry the reflections appear.

- **Normal Map:** A normal map simulates fine surface details by perturbing the surface normals. This gives the illusion of depth and adds realism to materials.

- **Metallic and Roughness:** These properties determine if a material is metallic (like metal) or dielectric (like plastic). Roughness controls the microsurface roughness of the material, affecting the sharpness of reflections.

Texture Maps

Texture maps are images that define material properties. To create realistic materials, you'll often use the following types of texture maps:

- **Diffuse (Albedo) Map:** This map defines the base color of the material.

- **Specular Map:** Used to control the intensity and color of reflections on the material's surface.

- **Normal Map:** Provides surface detail information, creating the illusion of bumps and crevices.

- **Metallic Map:** Specifies which parts of the material are metallic (1.0) and which are dielectric (0.0).

- **Roughness Map:** Determines the smoothness or roughness of the material's surface.

UV Mapping

UV mapping is the process of "unwrapping" a 3D model's surface onto a 2D plane, creating a map that associates each point on the surface with a corresponding point on a texture. Proper UV mapping is crucial for applying textures accurately to your 3D models.

Procedural Textures

In addition to texture maps, Godot allows you to create procedural textures using shaders. Procedural textures can be used for various effects, such as dynamic weathering, patterns, or unique visual styles.

Here's an example of creating a simple procedural noise texture in a shader:

```
shader_type canvas_item;

uniform float scale : hint_range(0.1, 10.0) = 1.0;

void fragment() {
    // Create a 2D noise pattern
    vec2 noise = noise(vec3(FRAGCOORD.xy * scale, 0.0));
```

```
    // Output the noise as color
    COLOR = vec4(noise, 0.0, 1.0);
}
```

PBR (Physically Based Rendering)

Godot follows the principles of Physically Based Rendering (PBR) to create realistic materials. PBR aims to simulate how light interacts with materials in the real world. Godot's PBR materials make it easier to create materials that respond realistically to lighting conditions.

Material Shaders

To achieve more complex and custom material effects, you can create material shaders in Godot. Material shaders allow you to write custom code to manipulate material properties dynamically.

In conclusion, creating realistic materials and textures in Godot is a vital aspect of game development, especially for 3D games. By understanding material properties, texture maps, UV mapping, procedural textures, and PBR principles, you can elevate the visual quality of your game and immerse players in a more convincing virtual world. Experiment with different textures and shaders to achieve the desired look and feel for your game's materials.

16.4 GPU-Based Effects and Shaders

In this section, we will explore the power of GPU-based effects and shaders in Godot. Shaders allow you to implement advanced graphical effects, manipulate visuals in real-time, and create stunning visuals that can set your game apart.

What Are Shaders?

Shaders are small programs that run directly on the GPU (Graphics Processing Unit). They are used to manipulate the appearance of objects, control lighting, and create various visual effects. In Godot, you can write shaders using the Shader Language (a variant of GLSL) or use the visual shader editor for simpler effects.

Types of Shaders

Godot supports several types of shaders, including:

- **CanvasItem Shaders:** These shaders affect 2D elements, such as sprites and user interface components.

- **Spatial Shaders:** Used for 3D objects, spatial shaders can create complex 3D effects like dynamic reflections, refractions, and more.

- **Particles Shaders:** Particles in Godot can also have custom shaders, enabling you to create unique particle effects.

Shader Language

Godot's Shader Language is a simplified version of GLSL (OpenGL Shading Language). While it is more accessible than writing raw GLSL code, it is still powerful and flexible.

16.5 Optimizing Render Performance for Complex Scenes

Optimizing render performance is a critical aspect of game development, especially when dealing with complex scenes in Godot. As your game world becomes more detailed and expansive, it's essential to ensure that it runs smoothly on players' devices. In this section, we'll explore various techniques and strategies to optimize render performance in Godot.

Level of Detail (LOD)

Level of Detail (LOD) is a technique used to reduce the rendering load by simplifying 3D models as they move away from the camera. In Godot, you can implement LOD by creating multiple versions of a model with varying levels of detail and switching between them based on the distance from the camera. This reduces the number of polygons rendered, improving performance.

Here's a simplified example of LOD in GDScript:

```
func _ready():
    # Create LOD models with decreasing complexity
    var high_detail = load("res://models/high_detail.gltf")
    var medium_detail = load("res://models/medium_detail.gltf")
    var low_detail = load("res://models/low_detail.gltf")

    # Add them as child nodes (assuming they have proper collision shapes)
    add_child(high_detail)
    add_child(medium_detail)
    add_child(low_detail)

    # Initialize LOD distances
    high_detail.lod_max_distance = 10.0
    medium_detail.lod_min_distance = 10.0
    medium_detail.lod_max_distance = 30.0
    low_detail.lod_min_distance = 30.0
```

Occlusion Culling

Occlusion culling is a technique that prevents rendering objects that are not visible to the camera. Godot provides built-in occlusion culling support, which automatically hides objects that are obstructed by other objects in the scene. Enabling occlusion culling can significantly reduce the number of objects that need to be rendered.

Batching

Batching is the process of combining multiple objects into a single mesh for rendering. Godot's geometry instancing feature allows you to efficiently batch objects with the same material and transform. This reduces the number of draw calls and can significantly improve rendering performance.

Multithreading

Godot 3.2 introduced multithreading support for rendering. Enabling the "Use multithreaded rendering" option in project settings can distribute rendering tasks across multiple CPU cores, improving rendering performance for scenes with many objects.

Proper Texturing

Texture sizes and formats can have a significant impact on rendering performance. Ensure that textures are appropriately sized for their usage. Use texture atlases to reduce the number of texture switches, and use compressed texture formats where suitable to save memory and improve loading times.

Culling and Frustum Checks

Godot performs automatic frustum culling to skip rendering objects that are outside the camera's view frustum. However, you can further optimize this by manually implementing additional culling checks based on the needs of your game. This can include culling objects based on distance, screen space, or other criteria.

Render Layers and Groups

Godot allows you to organize objects into render layers and groups. This can help you selectively render specific groups of objects, reducing rendering overhead when certain objects don't need to be visible or interacted with at a given moment.

Profiling and Debugging

Godot provides profiling tools that allow you to analyze rendering performance. Use these tools to identify performance bottlenecks, such as high GPU or CPU usage during rendering. Profiling can help you pinpoint areas that require optimization.

In conclusion, optimizing render performance in Godot is crucial for delivering a smooth and enjoyable gaming experience. By implementing techniques like LOD, occlusion culling, batching, multithreading, and proper texturing, you can ensure that your game runs efficiently even in complex and detailed scenes. Profiling and debugging tools are your allies in identifying and addressing rendering performance issues.

Chapter 17: Extensions and Plugins

17.1 Extending Godot with Custom Modules

In this section, we will explore the concept of creating custom modules to extend Godot's functionality. Custom modules allow you to integrate native code, written in languages like C++ or Rust, into your Godot projects. This opens up the possibility of creating custom nodes, resources, and plugins that can enhance your game development workflow.

What are Custom Modules?

Custom modules are external code libraries that can be loaded and used within the Godot game engine. These modules are typically written in languages like C++ or Rust and can provide additional functionality not available through GDScript or built-in engine features. Custom modules are compiled into dynamic link libraries (DLLs) or shared object files (SOs) that Godot can load at runtime.

Why Use Custom Modules?

There are several reasons to consider using custom modules in your Godot projects:

4. **Performance:** Custom modules can take advantage of low-level programming languages, allowing you to optimize performance-critical parts of your game.

Access to Third-Party Libraries:

17.2 Exploring Popular Godot Plugins

In this section, we will delve into some of the popular plugins available for Godot. These plugins are created by the Godot community and can significantly enhance your game development workflow by providing additional features and tools.

Plugin Installation

Before we explore specific plugins, it's essential to understand how to install and manage them in Godot. Follow these general steps to install a plugin:

5. **Download the Plugin:** Visit the plugin's repository or website to download the plugin files. Plugins typically come in the form of GDScript files or ZIP archives.

6. **Place the Plugin:** If the plugin is provided as a GDScript file, place it in your project's "addons" directory. If it's a ZIP archive, extract its contents into the "addons" directory.

7. **Enable the Plugin:** In the Godot editor, navigate to "Project" > "Project Settings" > "Plugins." Here, you can enable or disable installed plugins.

8. **Configure the Plugin:** Some plugins may have configuration settings that you can adjust through the "Project Settings" window or a dedicated plugin settings section.

Let's explore some of the popular Godot plugins and their functionalities:

9. **AutoTileSet:** AutoTileSet simplifies the creation of autotiles for 2D tilemaps. It provides an easy-to-use interface for creating autotile patterns and is incredibly helpful for tile-based game development.

10. **Godot Discord Rich Presence:** This plugin allows you to integrate Discord Rich Presence into your Godot games. It displays detailed information about the game that players are currently enjoying, such as the current scene or game status.

11. **Aseprite Importer:** If you use Aseprite for pixel art creation, this plugin enables you to import Aseprite files directly into Godot as scenes, animations, and sprites. It streamlines the workflow for pixel art games.

12. **Spine Runtime:** For developers using the Spine 2D animation tool, the Spine Runtime plugin offers seamless integration with Godot. It enables you to import and use Spine animations and characters within your projects.

13. **TileMap Collision Editor:** This plugin enhances the collision editing capabilities of the TileMap node. It provides a visual editor for defining collision shapes for tiles, making it easier to create complex collision layouts for 2D games.

14. **Godot OpenVR:** If you're interested in virtual reality (VR) development, the Godot OpenVR plugin allows you to create VR experiences using Godot. It supports various VR headsets and simplifies VR game development.

15. **Animation Player Tween:** This plugin extends Godot's AnimationPlayer node by adding more advanced tweening capabilities. It provides a user-friendly interface for creating complex animations and transitions.

16. **Camera 2D Shaker:** Camera shakes can add excitement to your game's action sequences. This plugin simplifies the process of adding camera shakes and screen effects to your 2D games.

17. **Asset Library Manager:** Managing assets in a Godot project can become challenging as it grows. This plugin helps organize and manage assets efficiently, including scenes, scripts, and resources.

18. **Godot Steam:** If you plan to publish your game on the Steam platform, the Godot Steam plugin provides a straightforward way to integrate Steamworks features, such as achievements, leaderboards, and multiplayer networking.

Community Contributions

The Godot community is active in creating and sharing plugins, and new plugins are continually being developed. Before choosing a plugin, consider your project's specific needs and look for community feedback and reviews to ensure the chosen plugin aligns with your goals.

Using plugins can significantly streamline your game development process and add features that would otherwise require substantial development effort. Experiment with different plugins to discover how they can enhance your workflow and improve your game development experience in Godot.

17.3 Creating and Sharing Your Own Plugins

In this section, we will explore the process of creating and sharing your own plugins for Godot. Developing custom plugins can be a powerful way to extend the functionality of the engine and share your solutions with the Godot community.

Why Create Your Own Plugins?

Creating your own plugins can be advantageous for several reasons:

19. **Custom Functionality:** You can implement specific features or tools tailored to your game project's needs that may not be available in existing plugins.

20. **Reuse and Efficiency:** Plugins allow you to reuse code and functionality across multiple projects, saving development time.

21. **Community Contribution:** Sharing your plugins with the Godot community can contribute to the growth and improvement of the engine.

Creating a Godot Plugin

To create a Godot plugin, follow these general steps:

22. **Design the Plugin:** Define the functionality and features of your plugin. Consider what problem it solves and how it integrates with Godot.

23. **Write the Code:** Develop the plugin's functionality using GDScript or a combination of GDScript and C++ (for more complex tasks). Ensure that your code is well-documented and follows best practices.

24. **Organize the Files:** Organize your plugin files into a structured directory. It should contain the plugin script(s), any required assets, and documentation.

25. **Create a Plugin Script:** In Godot, create a script that acts as an entry point for your plugin. This script should extend the `EditorPlugin` class and define various methods and properties.

26. **Implement Initialization:** In your plugin script, implement the _enter_tree and _exit_tree methods to initialize and clean up your plugin when it's enabled or disabled in the editor.

27. **Register the Plugin:** In the _enter_tree method, use the EditorInterface to register your plugin with the Godot editor.

28. **Test the Plugin:** Test your plugin thoroughly to ensure it works as expected in the Godot editor.

Example: Simple Custom Plugin

Here's a simplified example of a custom Godot plugin:

Plugin Script (my_custom_plugin.gd):

```
extends EditorPlugin

func _enter_tree():
    # Register the plugin with the editor
    add_custom_type("MyCustomNode", "Node", preload("res://addons/my_custom_p
lugin/my_custom_node.gd"), preload("res://icon.png"))

func _exit_tree():
    # Unregister the plugin
    remove_custom_type("MyCustomNode")

func _get_plugin_name():
    return "My Custom Plugin"

func _get_plugin_description():
    return "A custom plugin for Godot"
```

Custom Node Script (my_custom_node.gd):

```
extends Node

func _ready():
    print("My Custom Node is ready!")
```

Sharing

17.4 Integrating Third-Party Tools and Services

In this section, we'll explore the process of integrating third-party tools and services into your Godot projects. Leveraging external tools and services can enhance various aspects of your game, from analytics and monetization to multiplayer networking and more. Integration often involves using APIs or SDKs provided by these third-party providers.

Before integrating any third-party tool or service, it's crucial to identify the specific needs of your game project. Consider the following areas where integration might be beneficial:

29. **Analytics:** Integrate analytics tools to gather data on player behavior, track key performance indicators, and improve game design based on player insights.

30. **Monetization:** Implement ad networks or in-app purchase systems to generate revenue from your game.

31. **Social Features:** Integrate social media sharing, leaderboards, and multiplayer capabilities to enhance player engagement and retention.

32. **Cloud Services:** Use cloud services for features like cloud save, player data storage, or server hosting for multiplayer games.

33. **Authentication:** Implement authentication systems to secure user accounts and profiles.

34. **Advertisement:** If your game includes ads, integrate ad mediation platforms to optimize ad revenue.

35. **Distribution Platforms:** Prepare your game for distribution on specific platforms, such as Steam, Google Play, or the App Store, by following their integration guidelines.

Integration Steps

The integration process can vary depending on the tool or service you're incorporating into your Godot project. However, here are some general steps to guide you:

36. **Select the Tool or Service:** Choose the third-party tool or service that best fits your project's requirements. Ensure that it provides the necessary documentation and APIs for integration.

37. **Acquire Credentials:** Most integrations require API keys or access credentials. Obtain these from the third-party provider by signing up for their service.

38. **Read Documentation:** Carefully review the documentation and integration guides provided by the third-party provider. Familiarize yourself with the required API endpoints, SDKs, and usage instructions.

39. **Integrate the SDK or API:** Depending on the tool or service, you may need to integrate their SDK into your project. This often involves importing libraries or GDNative modules.

40. **Implement Functionality:** Write code in your Godot project to utilize the third-party tool or service's functionality. This may involve making API calls, handling responses, and integrating features like ads, analytics, or multiplayer components.

41. **Test Thoroughly:** Test the integration thoroughly to ensure that it works as expected. Verify that data is being transmitted correctly, and that any user-facing features function as intended.

42. **Handle Errors and Exceptions:** Implement error handling and exception handling to gracefully manage issues that may arise during integration, such as network errors or invalid credentials.

Common Integrations

Here are some common third-party integrations in Godot:

- **Ad Networks:** Integrating ad networks like AdMob or Chartboost for monetization through ads.

- **Analytics:** Implementing analytics tools like Google Analytics or Firebase Analytics to track user behavior.

- **Social Features:** Integrating social platforms like Facebook or Twitter for sharing and connecting with friends.

- **Multiplayer Networking:** Using multiplayer networking solutions like Photon, Nakama, or Firebase Realtime Database for online multiplayer functionality.

- **Authentication:** Incorporating authentication providers like Google Sign-In, Facebook Login, or Apple Sign In to allow users to sign in with their existing accounts.

- **Cloud Services:** Leveraging cloud services such as Amazon Web Services (AWS), Google Cloud, or Microsoft Azure for backend services, storage, and more.

Security and Privacy

When integrating third-party tools and services, consider security and privacy concerns. Ensure that you handle user data and credentials securely, and comply with any relevant data protection regulations, such as GDPR or CCPA. Always follow best practices for secure coding and data transmission.

Integrating third-party tools and services can expand the capabilities of your Godot game and enhance the player experience. However, it's essential to choose your integrations wisely, thoroughly test them, and prioritize the security and privacy of user data. By following integration guidelines and documentation provided by third-party providers, you can successfully enhance your game's functionality and reach.

17.5 Community Contributions and Open Source Development

In this section, we'll explore the significance of community contributions and open-source development in the context of Godot and game development. The Godot game engine thrives on the active involvement of its community, and open-source principles play a fundamental role in its evolution.

The Power of Open Source

Godot's open-source nature means that its source code is freely available for anyone to view, modify, and distribute. This openness has several advantages for both developers and the community:

43. **Transparency:** Open source allows developers to inspect the engine's source code, providing a deep understanding of how it works. This transparency is invaluable for troubleshooting, optimization, and learning.

44. **Accessibility:** Godot's open-source nature ensures that game development is accessible to a broader audience. Anyone can download and use the engine without cost.

45. **Community Collaboration:** Open source fosters a vibrant community of contributors who actively engage in improving the engine. This collaborative effort leads to rapid development and bug fixes.

46. **Customization:** Developers can customize Godot to suit their specific project requirements, whether it's adding features, optimizing performance, or creating plugins.

How to Contribute

Contributing to the Godot project is open to anyone, regardless of their level of expertise. Here are some ways to get involved:

47. **Code Contributions:** If you're proficient in programming, you can contribute by fixing bugs, adding new features, or optimizing existing code. Fork the Godot repository on platforms like GitHub, make your changes, and submit pull requests.

Documentation: Improving documentation is crucial for making Godot more accessible.

Chapter 18: Game Design Principles

18.1 Core Concepts in Game Design

Game design is a multidisciplinary field that involves creating interactive experiences that engage and entertain players. It encompasses various elements, from gameplay mechanics and storytelling to user interface design and player psychology. In this section, we'll delve into the core concepts and principles of game design that every game developer should understand.

Player-Centered Design

One of the fundamental principles of game design is player-centered design. This means putting the player's experience and enjoyment at the forefront of your design decisions. Understanding your target audience, their preferences, and their expectations is essential for creating a game that resonates with players.

Gameplay Mechanics

Gameplay mechanics are the rules and systems that govern how a game is played. These mechanics include movement, combat, puzzles, resource management, and more. Effective game design involves designing mechanics that are intuitive, balanced, and enjoyable to engage with. Iteration and playtesting are essential to refine and optimize gameplay mechanics.

Player Agency

Player agency refers to the player's ability to make meaningful choices that impact the game's outcome. Games with high player agency often offer branching narratives, multiple solutions to challenges, and a sense of player control. Providing meaningful choices can enhance player engagement and replayability.

Progression and Flow

Game designers carefully structure the progression of a game to maintain a state of flow—a state where players are fully immersed and focused on the game. Balancing the difficulty curve, providing clear goals, and rewarding player achievements are all part of creating a seamless and enjoyable player experience.

Balancing Gameplay and Mechanics

Balancing gameplay and mechanics is crucial for ensuring a fair and enjoyable experience. This involves adjusting the difficulty, fine-tuning character abilities, and addressing any exploits or overpowered strategies. Balance ensures that players are challenged without feeling frustrated.

Narrative and Storytelling

Narrative is a powerful tool in game design. It can immerse players in a rich fictional world, create emotional connections with characters, and drive player motivation. Game designers use storytelling techniques to craft compelling narratives that enhance the overall gaming experience.

Designing Engaging Levels and Worlds

Level and world design play a significant role in game design. Well-designed levels provide a sense of progression, challenge, and exploration. Level designers consider pacing, environmental storytelling, and player guidance to create engaging and memorable experiences.

Player Psychology and Engagement Strategies

Understanding player psychology is key to keeping players engaged. Game designers leverage principles of motivation, reward systems, and behavioral psychology to create compelling gameplay loops and encourage player retention.

Iteration and Playtesting

Game design is an iterative process. Playtesting involves gathering feedback from players to identify strengths, weaknesses, and areas for improvement in your game. Regular playtesting and iteration help refine the gameplay experience and address any issues that arise.

Balancing Art and Functionality

Balancing art and functionality is essential for creating visually appealing and functional games. Art assets, animations, and user interface design should complement the gameplay and enhance the player's immersion.

In summary, game design is a complex and dynamic field that encompasses various disciplines and principles. Whether you're designing a simple mobile game or a complex AAA title, understanding these core concepts and applying them effectively is essential for creating games that captivate and entertain players. Game design is both an art and a science, requiring creativity, empathy, and a deep understanding of player behavior.

18.2 Balancing Gameplay and Mechanics

Balancing gameplay and mechanics is a critical aspect of game design that directly influences the player's experience. Game designers strive to create a balanced and enjoyable gameplay experience that challenges players without causing frustration. In this section, we'll explore the principles and techniques involved in balancing gameplay and mechanics.

The Importance of Balance

Game balance refers to the distribution and tuning of various elements within a game to ensure fair and engaging gameplay. Imbalanced games can lead to frustration or boredom, while balanced games provide a sense of challenge and accomplishment. Balance extends to multiple aspects of a game, including character abilities, item power, level difficulty, and more.

Types of Balance

48. **Character Balance:** In games with multiple playable characters or classes, it's crucial to balance their strengths and weaknesses. Each character should offer a unique playstyle without one being significantly more powerful than the others.

49. **Item and Equipment Balance:** Balancing the power and rarity of in-game items and equipment is essential. Overpowered items can trivialize challenges, while underpowered ones may discourage players.

50. **Difficulty Balance:** Game difficulty should progress gradually, allowing players to learn and adapt. Sudden spikes in difficulty can lead to frustration, while overly easy sections can lead to boredom.

51. **Resource Balance:** Managing resources like health, ammunition, or magic points is crucial. Players should face resource scarcity at times, but not to the extent that it impedes progress unfairly.

52. **Economy Balance:** In games with in-game economies, balancing the acquisition of currency or resources is vital. An imbalanced economy can lead to inflation or a lack of progression.

Techniques for Balancing

53. **Playtesting:** Regular playtesting with a diverse group of players is essential. Collect feedback on difficulty, balance, and any issues encountered during gameplay.

54. **Iterative Design:** Game designers should be prepared to make adjustments and refinements based on playtest feedback. Frequent iteration is key to achieving balance.

55. **Data Analysis:** Analyzing gameplay data can provide insights into player behavior and balance issues. Monitoring player statistics, such as win rates or item usage, can help identify imbalances.

56. **Mathematical Modeling:** Some games use mathematical models to calculate balance. For example, formulas can determine how damage scales with character attributes.

Balancing multiplayer games introduces additional challenges. In competitive multiplayer, imbalances can lead to frustration and may drive players away. Here are some considerations for balancing multiplayer games:

57. **Matchmaking:** Match players of similar skill levels to ensure fair competition.

58. **Regular Updates:** Continuously monitor and update the game to address balance issues and maintain a healthy player community.

59. **Community Feedback:** Engage with the player community to gather feedback on balance and address their concerns.

The Role of Player Feedback

Player feedback is invaluable for balancing gameplay and mechanics. Actively encourage players to provide feedback through in-game surveys, forums, or social media. A responsive approach to player feedback can lead to a more balanced and enjoyable game.

Case Study: "Overwatch" Hero Balancing

"Overwatch," a popular team-based shooter, provides an excellent case study in hero balancing. The game has a diverse cast of heroes, each with unique abilities. Blizzard Entertainment, the developer, regularly monitors hero usage, win rates, and community feedback. They adjust hero abilities, damage values, and other factors to maintain balance and ensure that no hero dominates the game.

Balancing gameplay and mechanics is an ongoing process in game design. It requires a combination of data analysis, player feedback, and design intuition. Striking the right balance is essential to create a game that challenges and engages players while providing a satisfying experience. Balancing is not a one-time task but a continuous effort that evolves with the player community and the changing dynamics of the game.

18.3 Narrative and Storytelling in Games

Narrative and storytelling are powerful tools in game design that can immerse players in a game's world, create emotional connections, and drive player motivation. In this section, we'll delve into the role of narrative and storytelling in games, exploring how they contribute to the overall gaming experience.

The Importance of Narrative

Narrative in games serves several critical purposes:

60. **Immersion:** A well-crafted narrative can immerse players in a game's world, making them feel like active participants in the story.

61. **Character Development:** Narratives allow for character development and evolution, creating relatable and memorable characters.

62. **Motivation:** A compelling narrative can provide players with clear goals and motivations for their in-game actions.

63. **Emotional Engagement:** Storytelling can evoke a wide range of emotions, from joy and excitement to sadness and empathy.

Types of Narrative in Games

Games employ various narrative structures and styles:

64. **Linear Narrative:** In linear narratives, the story progresses in a fixed sequence, and player choices have minimal impact on the overall plot. This approach is common in many single-player games, especially those with a strong focus on storytelling.

65. **Branching Narrative:** Branching narratives allow players to make choices that influence the storyline. These choices can lead to multiple endings or outcomes, providing a sense of agency.

66. **Open-Ended Narrative:** Some games offer open-ended narratives where players create their own stories within a sandbox or open-world environment. Games like "Minecraft" and "The Sims" fall into this category.

Game Storytelling Techniques

Effective storytelling in games involves several techniques:

67. **Dialogues:** Dialogues between characters convey information, emotions, and character traits. Well-written dialogues can enhance player engagement.

68. **Cutscenes:** Cutscenes are cinematic sequences that advance the story. They can provide essential context or showcase dramatic moments.

69. **Environmental Storytelling:** Game environments can tell stories through visual cues and details. For example, abandoned buildings and scattered notes can hint at a mysterious past.

70. **Character Arcs:** Characters should undergo development and change throughout the story, creating a sense of growth and progression.

71. **Pacing:** Proper pacing ensures that the story unfolds at a rhythm that keeps players engaged. Balancing action sequences with quieter moments is essential.

Balancing gameplay and storytelling is a challenge in game design. Gameplay should complement the narrative, and vice versa. Here are some strategies for achieving this balance:

72. **Integration:** Integrate story elements into gameplay mechanics. For example, a character's abilities might tie into their backstory or the game's lore.

73. **Player Agency:** Allow players to make choices that affect the story, but ensure these choices are meaningful and have consequences.

74. **Narrative Hooks:** Use narrative hooks to motivate players. Hooks are elements that pique players' curiosity and encourage them to explore and progress.

75. **Relevance:** Ensure that narrative elements are relevant to the gameplay. Players should see a connection between their actions and the story's progression.

Case Study: "The Last of Us"

"The Last of Us," developed by Naughty Dog, is known for its compelling narrative. The game blends cinematic storytelling with gameplay seamlessly. It follows the journey of Joel and Ellie as they navigate a post-apocalyptic world. The narrative is emotional, character-driven, and filled with moral dilemmas. Players become deeply attached to the characters and are motivated to complete the game not just for gameplay rewards but to see the story through to the end.

In summary, narrative and storytelling are integral components of game design that can elevate the player experience. Effective storytelling can immerse players in a game's world, drive motivation, and create emotional connections. Balancing gameplay and narrative is essential to ensure that both elements complement each other and contribute to an engaging and memorable gaming experience.

18.4 Designing Engaging Levels and Worlds

Level and world design are crucial aspects of game design that shape the player's experience. Well-designed levels provide a sense of progression, challenge, and exploration, while immersing players in the game's world. In this section, we'll explore the principles and techniques involved in designing engaging levels and worlds.

The Role of Level and World Design

76. **Progression:** Levels guide players through the game's story and challenges, providing a sense of progression and accomplishment.

77. **Challenge:** Well-designed levels gradually increase in difficulty, ensuring that players are challenged without feeling overwhelmed. The progression of challenges should align with the player's growing skills.

78. **Exploration:** Levels encourage exploration and discovery, rewarding players with hidden secrets, items, or narrative elements.

79. **Immersion:** Thoughtful world design immerses players in the game's setting, making it believable and captivating.

80. **Clear Goals:** Levels should provide clear objectives or goals for players. Whether it's reaching a destination, defeating a boss, or solving a puzzle, goals motivate players to progress.

81. **Pacing:** Pacing involves balancing moments of action, exploration, and downtime. It ensures that players are engaged but not overwhelmed.

82. **Variety:** Levels should offer variety in gameplay mechanics, environments, and challenges to keep players engaged and prevent repetition.

83. **Flow:** Flow refers to the feeling of being fully engaged and absorbed in the game. Well-designed levels maintain a state of flow, where players are focused and in control.

84. **Guidance:** Effective level design provides subtle guidance to direct players without holding their hands. This can be achieved through visual cues, environmental storytelling, or level layout.

Environmental Storytelling

Environmental storytelling is a technique where the game world and its details convey aspects of the narrative. It can involve:

- **Visual Clues:** Props, graffiti, or objects that tell a story or provide context.
- **Non-Playable Characters (NPCs):** NPCs can engage in conversations, offer quests, or provide information about the world.
- **Architecture and Layout:** The design of buildings and structures can communicate the history or purpose of a location.
- **Audio Design:** Background sounds, music, or ambient noise can enhance immersion and convey emotions.

Challenges and Puzzles

Well-designed levels often include challenges and puzzles that align with the game's mechanics and narrative. These can include platforming challenges, combat encounters, riddles, or logic puzzles. The difficulty of these challenges should be balanced to provide a sense of accomplishment upon completion.

Player-Driven Exploration

Encouraging player-driven exploration is essential for immersive level and world design. Here are some techniques:

- **Hidden Secrets:** Reward players for exploring by placing hidden secrets, items, or collectibles in the environment.
- **Non-Linear Paths:** Allow players to choose different paths or approaches to reach their objectives.
- **Backtracking:** Enable backtracking to previous areas with newfound abilities, revealing new opportunities or story elements.

Testing and Iteration

Playtesting is a critical part of level design. Gathering feedback from players helps identify issues, pacing problems, or areas of frustration. Iterating on level design based on player feedback is essential to creating engaging and polished levels.

Case Study: "Super Mario" Series

The "Super Mario" series, created by Nintendo, is renowned for its exceptional level design. Levels are designed to teach players new mechanics gradually, introducing challenges that build upon previously learned skills. The series' iconic power-ups, such as the Super Mushroom and Fire Flower, are strategically placed to provide players with moments of empowerment. The colorful and imaginative world design adds to the charm and immersion of the games.

In conclusion, level and world design are integral to creating engaging and immersive game experiences. Effective level design considers progression, challenge, exploration, and immersion. Balancing these elements, providing clear goals, and using environmental storytelling techniques contribute to memorable and enjoyable gameplay. Whether creating a platformer, action-adventure, or open-world game, thoughtful level and world design enhance the player's journey and overall satisfaction.

18.5 Player Psychology and Engagement Strategies

Understanding player psychology is crucial for designing games that captivate and retain players. Game designers often employ various psychological principles to create engaging gameplay experiences. In this section, we'll explore player psychology and the strategies that can be used to enhance player engagement.

Motivation is a fundamental aspect of player psychology. Games often use reward systems to motivate players to take specific actions or achieve particular goals. Key strategies include:

- **Progression Systems:** Games often incorporate progression systems where players earn experience points (XP) or unlock new abilities as they advance. This provides a sense of achievement and motivates players to continue playing.

- **Achievements and Trophies:** The prospect of earning achievements or trophies can be a powerful motivator. These virtual badges or rewards recognize a player's accomplishments and encourage completionists.

- **Unlockable Content:** Games may hide content behind progression, encouraging players to keep playing to access new levels, characters, or features.

Behavioral Psychology

Game designers also draw from behavioral psychology principles to create engaging experiences:

- **Positive Reinforcement:** Rewarding desired behaviors with positive feedback, such as points, sounds, or visual effects, encourages players to repeat those behaviors.

- **Variable Rewards:** Variable or unpredictable rewards, such as random loot drops or surprise bonuses, can be particularly compelling, as they trigger the brain's reward centers.

- **Loss Aversion:** Players often fear losing progress or valuable items more than they desire gaining new ones. Game mechanics that create a sense of loss aversion can keep players engaged.

- **Framing and Anchoring:** How information is presented can influence player decisions. Framing a task as a challenge rather than a chore can make it more appealing.

Player Retention

Player retention is a critical aspect of game design. Keeping players engaged over time requires strategies that address common challenges, including:

- **Onboarding:** A smooth onboarding process introduces new players to the game's mechanics gradually, reducing the barrier to entry.

- **Daily Rewards:** Providing daily rewards or incentives for returning to the game can establish a habit of play.

- **Events and Limited-Time Content:** Time-limited events, special challenges, or seasonal content can create a sense of urgency and encourage players to log in regularly.

- **Social Features:** Social elements, such as multiplayer modes, guilds, or leaderboards, can foster a sense of community and competition, increasing player retention.

The Power of Feedback

Feedback mechanisms, including audiovisual cues and haptic feedback, play a significant role in player engagement. Examples include:

- **Visual Feedback:** Visual effects, animations, and UI elements can communicate success, progress, or challenges to the player.

- **Auditory Feedback:** Sound effects, music changes, and voiceovers provide auditory cues that enhance the player's emotional response and understanding of the game.

- **Haptic Feedback:** Vibrations or force feedback in controllers or devices can create a tactile connection between the player and the game world.

Behavioral Economics

Behavioral economics principles, which explore how individuals make decisions, can be applied to game design:

- **Scarcity:** Creating a sense of scarcity, such as limited-time offers or rare in-game items, can drive player engagement as players seek to acquire these scarce resources.

- **Loss Aversion:** Players may be more motivated to act to avoid perceived losses than to gain equivalent rewards.

- **Anchoring:** Presenting players with initial reference points, such as high prices or challenging goals, can influence their perception of subsequent offers or achievements.

Ethical Considerations

While employing player psychology to enhance engagement is a common practice in game design, ethical considerations are essential. Game designers must strike a balance between creating engaging experiences and avoiding manipulative or exploitative practices. Ensuring that player engagement strategies are used responsibly and do not lead to harmful outcomes for players is a fundamental ethical responsibility in game design.

In conclusion, understanding player psychology is a powerful tool in creating engaging and enjoyable games. By applying principles from motivation, behavioral psychology, player retention, feedback mechanisms, behavioral economics, and maintaining ethical considerations, game designers can create experiences that resonate with players, keeping them engaged and entertained over time. Player psychology is an evolving field, and staying informed about the latest research and trends can help designers continue to improve their games and enhance player satisfaction.

Chapter 19: Marketing and Publishing

19.2 Building a Community and Engaging with Players

Building a community around your game is a vital aspect of successful game marketing and publishing. A dedicated player community can generate excitement, provide valuable feedback, and become strong advocates for your game. In this section, we'll explore strategies for building and engaging with your game's community.

Establishing

19.4 Monetization Strategies and Business Models

Choosing the right monetization strategy and business model for your game is a critical decision that can significantly impact its financial success and player satisfaction. In this section, we'll explore various monetization strategies and business models commonly used in the gaming industry.

Monetization Strategies

85. **One-Time Purchase (Premium):** In this model, players pay a fixed price to purchase the game upfront. This strategy is common for high-quality indie games and premium AAA titles. It provides an immediate source of revenue and allows developers to avoid free-to-play monetization tactics.

86. **Free-to-Play (F2P):** Free-to-play games are accessible without an initial purchase cost. Instead, revenue is generated through in-game purchases, such as virtual items, cosmetics, or currency. F2P games often offer optional microtransactions that enhance the player's experience or progression.

87. **Freemium:** Freemium games offer a combination of free content and optional premium features or content that players can purchase. This model allows players to enjoy the game without spending money while offering enticing paid options.

88. **Subscription:** Subscription-based models provide players with ongoing access to a game's content and features in exchange for a recurring fee. This approach is commonly used for massively multiplayer online games (MMOs) and services like Xbox Game Pass or Apple Arcade.

89. **Ads and Ad-Supported:** Games can generate revenue by displaying advertisements to players. Ad-supported games often provide an option to remove ads through a

one-time purchase or subscription. Interstitial ads, rewarded videos, and banner ads are common formats.

90. **In-App Purchases (IAPs):** In-app purchases allow players to buy virtual items, currency, or premium content within the game. These purchases can enhance gameplay or provide cosmetic items. Gacha systems, loot boxes, and cosmetic skins are popular IAPs.

Business Models

7. **DLC and Expansion Packs:** Downloadable content (DLC) and expansion packs offer additional content, such as new levels, characters, or storylines, for an existing game. This model extends the game's lifespan and provides a revenue stream beyond the initial release.

8. **Season Pass:** A season pass bundles multiple DLCs or expansions into a single purchase. Players receive all included content over a specified period, often at a discounted price compared to buying each DLC individually.

9. **Game as a Service (GaaS):** GaaS models focus on long-term player engagement and retention. Developers continuously release updates, events, and content expansions, often supported by in-game purchases, to keep players invested in the game over time.

10. **Crowdfunding:** Some indie developers and smaller studios use crowdfunding platforms like Kickstarter to raise funds for game development. Backers receive rewards or early access in exchange for their support.

Pay-What-

19.5 Post-Launch Support and Updates

Post-launch support and updates are crucial aspects of maintaining a successful game and keeping your player base engaged. Players expect ongoing improvements, bug fixes, and new content, and meeting these expectations can lead to long-term success and player loyalty. In this section, we'll explore the importance of post-launch support and strategies for effectively managing updates.

The Importance of Post-Launch Support

91. **Player Retention:** Post-launch support can help retain players by providing fresh content, fixing issues, and enhancing the overall gaming experience. A dedicated player base is more likely to recommend your game to others.

92. **Positive Reviews:** Addressing player feedback and improving your game can lead to positive reviews and word-of-mouth marketing. Happy players are more likely to leave favorable reviews on platforms like Steam or app stores.

93. **Monetization Opportunities:** Post-launch updates can introduce new monetization opportunities, such as additional content or in-game purchases. This can generate revenue beyond the initial game sale.

94. **Community Engagement:** Continuously supporting your game keeps the community engaged. Players appreciate developers who listen to their feedback and actively work to improve the game.

Strategies for Effective Post-Launch Support

5. **Regular Updates:** Commit to a schedule of regular updates to keep players engaged. Whether it's weekly, monthly, or seasonally, consistency in updates helps maintain player interest.

6. **Bug Fixes and Quality Assurance:** Prioritize bug fixes and quality assurance to ensure a stable and enjoyable gaming experience. Address critical issues promptly to avoid frustrating players.

7. **Player Feedback:** Actively seek player feedback through forums, social media, and surveys. Use this feedback to identify areas for improvement and prioritize updates accordingly.

8. **Content Expansion:** Introduce new content, such as levels, characters, skins, or features, to keep the game fresh. Content updates can re-engage existing players and attract new ones.

9. **Community Events:** Host in-game events, challenges, or competitions to encourage player participation and foster a sense of community. These events can be tied to special rewards or achievements.

10. **Seasonal Updates:** Consider seasonal updates or themed events that align with holidays or special occasions. Seasonal content can create excitement and a sense of timeliness.

Communication with Players

11. **Transparency:** Be transparent with your player community about your post-launch plans and updates. Share roadmaps, patch notes, and development insights to build trust.

12. **Official Channels:** Use official communication channels, such as your game's website, social media profiles, and forums, to keep players informed about updates and events.

13. **Developer Blogs:** Consider publishing developer blogs or articles that provide insights into your development process, challenges, and the reasoning behind specific updates or changes.

14. **Community Feedback:** Acknowledge and respond to player feedback, both positive and negative. Engage with your community in a respectful and constructive manner.

Monetization in Post-Launch Updates

15. **Monetization Integration:** Introduce new monetization options in post-launch updates, such as additional in-game purchases, cosmetic items, or expansion packs. Ensure that monetization aligns with player expectations and provides value.

16. **Free vs. Paid Updates:** Carefully balance free and paid content updates. Offering free updates can maintain a healthy player base, while paid updates can generate revenue to support ongoing development.

17. **Loyalty Rewards:** Reward loyal players with exclusive content, discounts, or early access to updates. Recognizing and appreciating your dedicated player base can strengthen their connection to the game.

Version Compatibility

18. **Platform Updates:** Stay informed about platform-specific updates, patches, or changes that may affect your game's compatibility. Keep your game up to date to ensure a smooth experience for players.

19. **Cross-Platform Play:** If your game supports cross-platform play, ensure that updates are synchronized across all platforms to maintain a fair and consistent gaming experience.

Analytics and Player Data

20. **Analytics Tools:** Use analytics tools to track player engagement, retention, and behavior. Analyze data to understand which updates are most effective and inform your future development decisions.

21. **Player Surveys:** Conduct player surveys to gather feedback on specific updates or features. Player input can guide your development direction and help prioritize future updates.

In summary, post-launch support and updates are essential for the long-term success of your game. By consistently engaging with your player community, addressing their feedback, introducing new content, and maintaining transparency, you can build a dedicated player base and ensure the ongoing success of your game. Monetization opportunities within updates should be carefully integrated to provide value and enhance the player experience. Keeping your game fresh and exciting through regular updates is a key strategy in today's competitive gaming market.

20.1 Emerging Technologies in Game Development

Game development is a dynamic field that continually evolves with advancements in technology. Staying up-to-date with emerging technologies is crucial for game developers to create innovative and engaging experiences. In this section, we'll explore some of the emerging technologies that are shaping the future of game development.

Virtual Reality (VR) and Augmented Reality (AR)

95. **VR Gaming:** Virtual reality has gained significant attention in recent years, offering immersive gaming experiences. VR headsets, like Oculus Rift and HTC Vive, provide players with a sense of presence in virtual worlds. Game developers are creating VR titles that range from simulations to action-packed adventures.

96. **AR Integration:** Augmented reality overlays digital elements on the real world. Games like Pokémon GO introduced AR to a massive audience. AR glasses and mobile devices with AR capabilities open up new opportunities for game developers to create interactive and location-based experiences.

Cloud Gaming

3. **Cloud Streaming Services:** Cloud gaming services like Google Stadia, NVIDIA GeForce NOW, and Xbox Cloud Gaming (formerly Project xCloud) allow players to stream games over the internet. This technology reduces hardware limitations, enabling players to access high-quality gaming experiences on various devices.

4. **Cross-Platform Play:** Cloud gaming promotes cross-platform play by providing a consistent experience across devices. Game developers can tap into a larger player base and create seamless multiplayer experiences.

Ray Tracing and Realistic Graphics

5. **Ray Tracing:** Ray tracing is a rendering technique that simulates the behavior of light, resulting in highly realistic graphics. Graphics cards with ray tracing capabilities enable game developers to create lifelike lighting, reflections, and shadows.

6. **Real-Time Rendering:** Real-time ray tracing enhances visual fidelity, making games more immersive. Developers are exploring ray tracing in various game genres, from first-person shooters to open-world adventures.

Artificial Intelligence (AI)

7. **NPC Behavior:** AI-driven non-player characters (NPCs) are becoming more sophisticated. NPCs can exhibit lifelike behaviors, adapt to player actions, and contribute to dynamic gameplay experiences.

8. **Procedural Content Generation:** AI algorithms can generate game content, such as levels, environments, and quests, procedurally. This technology reduces development time and offers endless possibilities for game worlds.

5G Connectivity

9. **Low Latency Gaming:** 5G networks provide ultra-low latency, enabling smoother online gaming experiences. Developers can create real-time multiplayer games with minimal lag, enhancing competitive gaming.

10. **Remote Play:** With 5G, remote play becomes more accessible. Players can stream games from their home PCs or consoles to mobile devices, allowing for gaming on the go.

Blockchain and NFTs

11. **Blockchain Integration:** Blockchain technology is being explored for its potential in gaming. It can be used for digital asset ownership, secure item trading, and player-driven economies within games.

12. **Non-Fungible Tokens (NFTs):** NFTs are unique digital assets that represent ownership of in-game items or content. They have gained popularity for their potential to create rare and valuable in-game items.

Haptic Feedback and Immersive Sound

13. **Haptic Feedback:** Advanced haptic feedback systems in controllers provide tactile sensations, enhancing immersion. Players can feel vibrations, textures, and feedback that correspond to in-game actions.

14. **Immersive Audio:** Spatial audio technologies like Dolby Atmos and DTS:X provide immersive soundscapes. Game developers can create realistic audio experiences that enhance gameplay and storytelling.

Quantum Computing

15. **Simulation and Physics:** Quantum computing's immense processing power can be harnessed for complex simulations and physics calculations in games. This could lead to more realistic and dynamic virtual worlds.

16. **Encryption and Security:** Quantum-resistant encryption may become necessary to protect player data and in-game assets in the future.

Biofeedback and Player Interaction

17. **Biometric Data:** Games are beginning to incorporate biometric data from wearables and sensors to adapt gameplay based on a player's heart rate, stress levels, or other physiological factors.

18. **Emotional AI:** AI-driven systems can analyze player emotions through voice and facial recognition, enabling more personalized and emotionally responsive gaming experiences.

Sustainability and Green Gaming

19. **Environmental Considerations:** Game developers are increasingly aware of the environmental impact of their creations. Efforts are being made to reduce carbon footprints and promote green gaming practices.

20. **Eco-Friendly Initiatives:** From eco-friendly game development studios to energy-efficient game servers, the industry is making strides toward sustainability.

Emerging technologies are transforming the landscape of game development. Developers who embrace these technologies can create cutting-edge experiences that captivate players and push the boundaries of interactive entertainment. Staying informed about these trends and experimenting with their integration can lead to exciting and groundbreaking game projects in the years to come.

20.2 Keeping Up with Industry Trends

In the ever-evolving landscape of game development, keeping up with industry trends is not just an option; it's a necessity. Staying informed about the latest developments, technologies, and player preferences is essential for creating successful and relevant games. Here are some strategies and areas to consider when it comes to staying up-to-date with industry trends:

Attend Conferences and Events

97. **Game Developer Conferences:** Attending industry events like the Game Developers Conference (GDC) can provide valuable insights into emerging trends, technologies, and best practices. These conferences often feature sessions, panels, and networking opportunities with industry experts.

98. **Local Meetups and Workshops:** Check for local game development meetups and workshops. These events offer a more accessible way to connect with fellow developers and learn about regional trends and opportunities.

Follow Industry News and Publications

5. **Game Industry Websites:** Regularly visit game industry news websites and publications like Gamasutra, Kotaku, Polygon, and IGN. These sources cover a wide range of topics, from industry trends to game reviews and developer interviews.

6. **Developer Blogs and Journals:** Many game developers maintain blogs or write in-depth articles about their experiences and insights. These personal accounts can provide valuable perspectives on industry trends and challenges.

Engage on Social Media

5. **Twitter and Reddit:** Twitter is a popular platform for game developers to share their thoughts and discoveries. Follow industry professionals, game studios, and relevant hashtags to stay in the loop. Subreddits like r/gamedev are also valuable for discussions and insights.

6. **LinkedIn and Discord:** Join LinkedIn groups and Discord servers related to game development. These platforms offer a space for discussions, networking, and sharing of industry news.

7. **Play New Releases:** Playing a variety of games, especially recent releases, is essential. It helps you understand current player preferences, gameplay mechanics, and design trends. Analyze both successful and less successful titles to learn from their strengths and weaknesses.

8. **Game Analytics:** If you're a developer, consider using game analytics tools to gather data on player behavior in your own games. Analyzing this data can provide insights into what aspects of your game are engaging players and what might need improvement.

9. **Side Projects:** Work on side projects or game jams to experiment with new ideas and technologies. These small-scale projects can serve as testing grounds for innovative concepts and help you build skills.

10. **Collaborate with Others:** Collaborating with other developers, artists, and designers can expose you to different perspectives and skills. Joint projects often lead to new ideas and approaches.

11. **Experiment with VR/AR:** Even if you're not currently developing VR or AR games, experimenting with these technologies can provide valuable insights. VR headsets and AR apps are becoming more accessible, making it easier to explore their potential.

12. **Cloud Gaming Services:** Try out cloud gaming services like Google Stadia, NVIDIA GeForce NOW, and Xbox Cloud Gaming to understand their impact on game distribution and access.

13. **Online Courses:** Enroll in online courses and tutorials focused on game development. Platforms like Coursera, Udemy, and Unity Learn offer a wide range of courses, from beginner to advanced levels.

20.3 Participating in Game Jams and Competitions

Game jams and competitions are valuable opportunities for game developers to challenge themselves, spark creativity, and gain recognition within the industry. These events typically involve creating a game within a set timeframe, often with specific themes or constraints. Participating in game jams and competitions can offer numerous benefits:

Rapid Skill Development

Time Constraints: Game jams force developers to work under tight deadlines, which can lead to rapid skill development.

20.4 Continuing Education and Skill Development

Game development is a constantly evolving field, and to excel in it, you must commit to continuous learning and skill development. Even experienced developers can benefit from expanding their knowledge and staying up-to-date with the latest tools, technologies, and best practices. In this section, we'll explore various strategies for continuing your education and enhancing your skills as a game developer:

Online Courses and Tutorials

99. **Enroll in Online Courses:** Platforms like Coursera, Udemy, edX, and Pluralsight offer a wide range of online courses on game development topics. Whether you're a beginner or an experienced developer, you can find courses tailored to your needs.

20.5 Building a Career in Game Development with Godot

Building a career in game development with Godot, or any game engine, is an exciting journey that requires dedication, creativity, and a strong foundation of skills. In this section, we'll explore the steps you can take to establish and advance your career in the game development industry, specifically focusing on Godot Engine:

1. Master Godot Engine

To excel in Godot game development, you must become proficient in using the engine's features, including scene management, scripting in GDScript, 2D and 3D game development, physics, and more. Start with the basics and gradually work your way to more advanced topics. Online courses, tutorials, and Godot's official documentation are excellent resources for learning.

2. Create a Portfolio

Building a strong portfolio is crucial to showcasing your skills and attracting potential employers or clients. Develop a variety of games and projects using Godot to demonstrate your abilities. Include detailed project descriptions, gameplay videos, and downloadable demos to make your portfolio stand out.

3. Collaborate and Network

Game development often involves collaboration with others. Join game development communities, forums, and social media groups related to Godot to connect with fellow developers, artists, and designers. Collaboration can lead to valuable learning experiences and career opportunities.

4. Contribute to Open Source

Consider contributing to open source Godot projects. This not only allows you to give back to the community but also demonstrates your commitment and expertise in using the engine. It can also help you establish your reputation within the Godot community.

5. Attend Game Jams and Competitions

Participating in game jams and competitions, especially those focused on Godot, is an excellent way to test your skills, gain recognition, and expand your portfolio. It also provides a platform to connect with potential employers or collaborators.

6. Seek Internships or Entry-Level Positions

If you're starting your career, look for internships or entry-level positions in game development studios that use Godot or similar engines. These positions provide practical experience, mentorship, and a foot in the door.

7. Freelance and Independent Development

Consider freelance work or independent game development. Creating your games or offering your Godot expertise as a freelancer can help you gain experience, earn income, and build your reputation. Platforms like itch.io and Steam provide avenues for indie game distribution.

8. Continuous Learning

The game development industry is dynamic, with new technologies and trends emerging regularly. Stay up-to-date with Godot updates and industry developments. Continuously expand your skills, whether it's in areas like 3D graphics, AI programming, or VR/AR development.

9. Build a Personal Brand

Establishing a personal brand as a Godot developer can help you stand out in a competitive field. Create a professional website or blog, share your insights and experiences, and engage with the community through social media.

10. Create a Professional Resume and LinkedIn Profile

Craft a polished resume and LinkedIn profile that highlight your skills, projects, and achievements in the game development industry. Ensure that your portfolio and references are easily accessible.

11. Attend Conferences and Industry Events

Participate in game development conferences, workshops, and conventions to network with industry professionals, learn about the latest trends, and gain exposure to potential employers or clients.

12. Apply for Game Development Jobs

When you feel confident in your skills and experience, start applying for game development jobs. Look for positions that align with your interests and expertise, whether it's game design, programming, art, or other roles.

13. Be Persistent and Patient

Building a career in game development can be challenging, and success may not come overnight. Stay persistent, keep refining your skills, and don't be discouraged by setbacks. Continuously seek opportunities for growth and improvement.

Remember that the game development industry values passion, creativity, and dedication. As you work on projects and collaborate with others, your experience and reputation will grow, opening doors to exciting opportunities in the world of game development with Godot Engine.

www.ingramcontent.com/pod-product-compliance
Lightning Source LLC
LaVergne TN
LVHW051703050326
832903LV00032B/3979